ENDORSEMENTS FOR *IT'S TIME TO TALK: A WOMAN'S GUIDE TO NAVIGATING MONEY CONVERSATIONS*

"A must-read for every woman. **It's Time to Talk** is more than a guide to money. It's a guide to owning our voice, our choices, and our future. Sheila Schroeder writes with the wisdom of experience and the heart of a good friend who knows exactly what she's talking about when it comes to financial wisdom."

—**Sharon Kedar**, Co-Founder, Northpond Ventures

"Sheila Schroeder's groundbreaking book is a blueprint for women who seek agency over their financial narratives – an essential ingredient for true autonomy. Economic empowerment is inseparable from the ability to make decisions about our own bodies and lives. By opening up the conversation around money, Schroeder's work gives women the tools to claim both financial and personal freedom. This is a powerful resource for anyone committed to advancing women's equality in every sphere."

—**Nancy Northup**, President and CEO, Center for Reproductive Rights

"An indispensable tool kit which I plan to give to women on the cusp of new beginnings - fresh graduates, new moms and professionals on the rise."
"This book should come with a multi-colored pack of highlighters."

—**Sarah Dyer**, Co-founder, 100 Women in Finance

"Talking about money is uncomfortable, but avoiding these conversations is Ruinous Empathy, and is both financially and emotionally disastrous. Schroeder's liberating advice will help you be radically candid about money."

—**Kim Scott**, Author of *Radical Candor*

"As someone who has had thousands of conversations about wealth with my own clients, I can say **It's Time To Talk** is a book that can empower any woman to feel confident in starting and being part of any conversation about money. It is perfectly pitched and delivered with compassion and authenticity, which speaks volumes about Sheila's natural ability to connect women to this vital narrative."

—**Kristen Cunneliffe**, DipPFS CeFC; Specialist Financial Educator & Personal Financial Coach in Elite Sport

"Sheila Schroeder changed our lives when she taught our family – including our kids – how to talk to each other about the topic most families avoid: money. Now, in this stunningly fresh book, she shares her bring-down-the-walls strategies in simple, step-by-step lessons that anyone can understand. Even men."

—**Phillip Lerman**, Best-selling author and former national editor of USA Today

"In this book, **It's Time to Talk: A Woman's Guide to Navigating Money Conversations**, Sheila masterfully combines decades of financial expertise with real-life, relatable guidance to help women step into their power around money. This book is not just about financial literacy, it's about breaking through societal conditioning, building true financial confidence, and learning how to navigate even the toughest money conversations with grace and authenticity. If you are ready to take ownership of your financial future and develop the confidence to talk about money in any setting, whether at home, in the workplace, or in your personal relationships, this book will be your trusted guide. Sheila's heart, experience, and wisdom leap off every page. I cannot recommend this book highly enough."

—**Trevor McGregor**, High-Performance Coach, Business Strategist and Real Estate Investor

"*Confidence in money conversations matters as much at home as it does at work. It's Time to Talk equips women to navigate them with clarity, courage, and purpose—whoever is on the other side of the table.*"
—**Carolyn Dewar**, New York Times bestselling co-author of CEO Excellence and the upcoming *A CEO for All Seasons*, and advisor to senior leaders around the world

"*In **It's Time to Talk: A Woman's Guide to Navigating Money Conversations**, Sheila Schroeder delivers a refreshingly candid and empowering guide that encourages women to confront financial topics with confidence and clarity. With warmth and wisdom, Sheila dismantles the fear and stigma often surrounding money discussions, showing how strong communication skills are the gateway to financial literacy and self-empowerment.*"
—**Heather Flanagan**, Managing Director, Head of Family Office Services, Wealthspire Advisors

IT'S TIME TO TALK

A WOMAN'S GUIDE TO NAVIGATING MONEY CONVERSATIONS

SHEILA SCHROEDER

WILEY

Copyright © 2026 Sheila Schroeder. All rights reserved.

Published by John Wiley & Sons, Inc., Hoboken, New Jersey.

No part of this publication may be reproduced, stored in a retrieval system, or transmitted in any form or by any means, electronic, mechanical, photocopying, recording, scanning, or otherwise, except as permitted under Section 107 or 108 of the 1976 United States Copyright Act, without either the prior written permission of the Publisher, or authorization through payment of the appropriate per-copy fee to the Copyright Clearance Center, Inc., 222 Rosewood Drive, Danvers, MA 01923, (978) 750-8400, fax (978) 750-4470, or on the web at www.copyright.com. Requests to the Publisher for permission should be addressed to the Permissions Department, John Wiley & Sons, Inc., 111 River Street, Hoboken, NJ 07030, (201) 748-6011, fax (201) 748-6008, or online at http://www.wiley.com/go/permission.

The manufacturer's authorized representative according to the EU General Product Safety Regulation is Wiley-VCH GmbH, Boschstr. 12, 69469 Weinheim, Germany, e-mail: Product_Safety@wiley.com.

Trademarks: Wiley and the Wiley logo are trademarks or registered trademarks of John Wiley & Sons, Inc. and/or its affiliates in the United States and other countries and may not be used without written permission. All other trademarks are the property of their respective owners. John Wiley & Sons, Inc. is not associated with any product or vendor mentioned in this book.

Limit of Liability/Disclaimer of Warranty: While the publisher and the authors have used their best efforts in preparing this work, including a review of the content of the work, neither the publisher nor the authors make any representations or warranties with respect to the accuracy or completeness of the contents of this work and specifically disclaim all warranties, including without limitation any implied warranties of merchantability or fitness for a particular purpose. No warranty may be created or extended by sales representatives, written sales materials or promotional statements for this work. The fact that an organization, website, or product is referred to in this work as a citation and/or potential source of further information does not mean that the publisher and authors endorse the information or services the organization, website, or product may provide or recommendations it may make. This work is sold with the understanding that the publisher is not engaged in rendering professional services. The advice and strategies contained herein may not be suitable for your situation. You should consult with a specialist where appropriate. Further, readers should be aware that websites listed in this work may have changed or disappeared between when this work was written and when it is read. Neither the publisher nor authors shall be liable for any loss of profit or any other commercial damages, including but not limited to special, incidental, consequential, or other damages.

For general information on our other products and services or for technical support, please contact our Customer Care Department within the United States at (800) 762-2974, outside the United States at (317) 572-3993 or fax (317) 572-4002.

Wiley also publishes its books in a variety of electronic formats. Some content that appears in print may not be available in electronic formats. For more information about Wiley products, visit our web site at www.wiley.com.

Library of Congress Cataloging-in-Publication Data has been applied for:

Hardback ISBN: 9781394380817
ePDF ISBN: 9781394380831
ePub ISBN: 9781394380824

Cover Design: Wiley
Cover Image: © johavel/Getty Images

Set in 11/16 Minion Pro Regular by Lumina Datamatics
SKY10130145_103025

DISCLAIMER

The information provided in this book is for informational and educational purposes only and is not intended to be a source of advice or analysis with respect to the material presented. The information and documents contained in this book do not constitute legal or financial advice and should never be used without first consulting with a financial professional to determine what may be best for your individual needs. The publisher and the author do not make any guarantee or other promise as to any results that may be obtained from using the content of this book. You should never make any investment decision without first consulting with your own financial advisor and conducting your own research and due diligence. To the maximum extent permitted by law, the publisher and the author disclaim any and all liability in the event any information, commentary, analysis, opinions, advice, and/or recommendations contained in this book prove to be inaccurate, incomplete, or unreliable or result in any investment or other losses. Content contained or made available through this book is not intended to and does not constitute investment or legal advice, and no client relationship is formed by reading this content. The publisher and the author are providing this book and its contents on an "as is" basis. Your use of the information in this book is at your own risk.

To my three favorite people

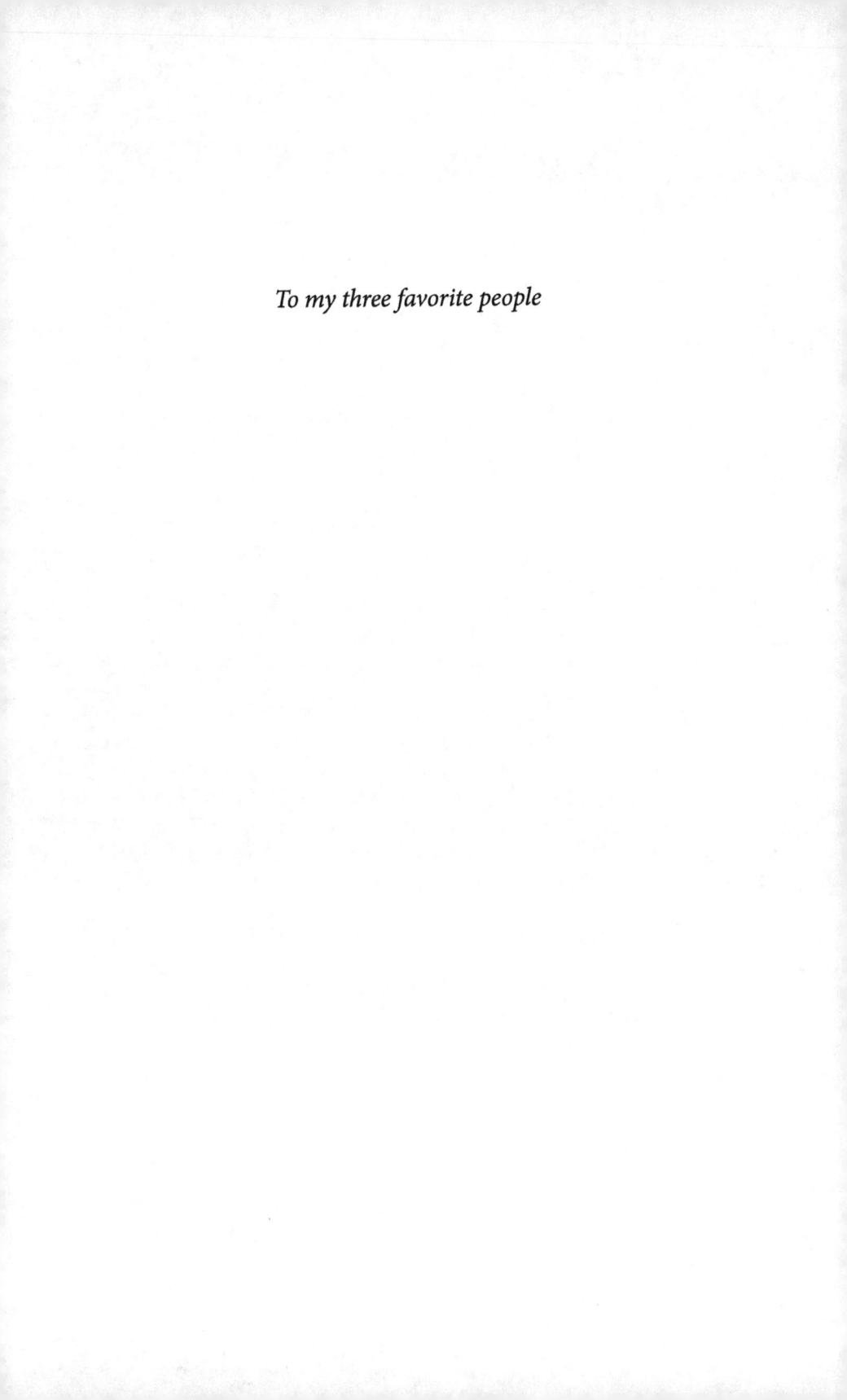

"There's only one very good life, and that's the life you know you want, and you make it yourself."
– Diana Vreeland

CONTENTS

INTRODUCTION 1

PART I
MONEY TALKS: BUILDING YOUR FINANCIAL FLUENCY 11

CHAPTER 1
    MASTERING THE BASICS: CREDIT, SAVINGS, AND AN EMERGENCY FUND 13

CHAPTER 2
    DREAMING BIG: A FUTURE THAT INSPIRES YOU 29

CHAPTER 3
    FROM DREAMING TO BUDGETING: A CONCRETE PLAN 41

CHAPTER 4
    TAKING A RISK: INVESTMENT AND DEBT 57

CHAPTER 5
    MAKING A MARK: GIVING TO CHARITIES AND POLITICAL CAUSES 75

PART II
TALKING MONEY: NAVIGATING FINANCES IN YOUR RELATIONSHIPS 85

CHAPTER 6
    MONEY CONVERSATIONS 101 87

CONTENTS

CHAPTER 7
YOUR MONEY TEAM — 107

CHAPTER 8
YOUR MONEY AND YOUR BOSS — 123

CHAPTER 9
BUILDING A FINANCIALLY SOUND MARRIAGE — 145

CHAPTER 10
RAISING MONEY-CONFIDENT KIDS — 163

CHAPTER 11
STAYING WHOLE WHEN YOU SPLIT UP — 181

CHAPTER 12
YOUR MONEY, AGING, AND LEGACY TALKS — 199

CHAPTER 13
DEALING WITH DEATH — 219

EPILOGUE — 239
APPENDIX (CHAPTER 9) — 249
MORE RESOURCES — 255
ACKNOWLEDGMENTS — 257
ABOUT THE AUTHOR — 259
INDEX — 261

INTRODUCTION

"You always have to have your own money," my mother said to me one evening when I was in my late twenties. Her tone made clear that this was no casual comment. It came from the depth of her experience—and it addressed what she knew had been considerable pain on my part.

Throughout my childhood, my mother had refrained from such strong pronouncements, and she had often deferred to my father on all manner of topics. But we were discussing one particularly hurtful area: discipline. In my adolescence, I had been a mouthy, opinionated kid who pushed the edge of what my parents considered acceptable behavior. I wanted to stay out late with friends and often talked back—in other words, I was a typical teenager.

But my father was a strict man with a temper, raised with the dictum *Spare the rod, spoil the child*. He did not spare the rod with me. If he was displeased with me (which he often was), he hit me with a belt. He never hit my mother or my sister; just me.

I don't want to paint my father as a villain. He grew up on a farm in northern Indiana and built a life for us from a modest beginning. Later on, he was supportive of my career and proud of me. He was the guy who would go out in the middle of the night in the pouring rain to help you change a flat tire. I see him as a product of his time, doing what he thought was right and practicing what for many people was a standard child rearing method: corporal punishment. He was a good but flawed man, and I have long since forgiven him.

Still, the experience of being punished that way affected me deeply. It instilled in me an anti-authoritarian streak, and it left emotional scars I have had to work hard to heal.

That evening in my twenties, I had worked up the courage to talk to my mother about her acquiescence to my father. Why had she allowed this to go on? After all, from the beginning, my mother had challenged societal norms. She was the youngest daughter from a traditional family in southern Japan. In the 1950s, she moved to Tokyo, studied English, and got a job. She met my American dad when they worked at the same company; they got married at the American embassy and built a life together—first in Japan, then in Taiwan and the United States. She had left her hometown for a bigger life, married a foreigner, moved abroad, and worked outside the home because she cared about her independence. It was important for her to be her own woman. Yet, when my dad was disciplining me, she didn't step in.

That night, I asked her, "How could you have let that happen?" I couldn't imagine standing by and watching my husband hit my kids. Hit anyone.

She apologized. "I should have said something," she told me. "But what was I going to do? Move back to Japan? Leave your father?"

She simply did not believe it was an option for her to contradict him when I was younger. Instead, that night she offered her firm admonition: "You always have to have your own money." Yes, my mother had had a job—but not enough money to pick up and leave. If she had really been fully in control financially, if she really had had a choice, she might have made a different decision on my behalf.

But that is speculation. What's more important is what I took away from that night: I had to have enough money to support myself, so that someone else could never be the boss of me. Even before this conversation with my mother, from an early age I had understood that money meant power. I started with little jobs when I was nine, taking care of our neighbor's cat and selling Christmas cards door to door. Later, I substituted for our paperboy when he went on vacation and became an in-demand babysitter. I first paid taxes at age 15. When I wanted to go to a private high school, I juggled three jobs to pay my half of the tuition.

And when my father was hitting me—and later in high school, when he stopped, and would ground me constantly as punishment—I got a job at McDonald's to get away from the house. I wanted to get farther away when I graduated. Money was going to help get me there.

Of course, I made missteps. At 17, as a junior in high school, I accidentally got pregnant. It was the first time I'd ever had sex. (It happens. We are very fertile at 17!) I was scared. This was deeply at odds with my plans to go to college, travel the world, move to the big city, and escape.

At the all-girls Catholic school I attended (though I was raised Protestant), girls got pregnant all the time. It was under the radar, but we knew. We knew which girls' parents had made them have their babies, which parents made sure their daughters had access to birth control, even the basic mechanics of how it all worked when someone went away for a procedure. That we knew was my first hint about the power of women's whisper networks, the way women support each other beyond the watchful eyes of people in authority.

This was 1978, five years after *Roe vs. Wade*. My abortion was not a difficult decision, and I was grateful I could make the choice. I don't remember how much it cost, but it wasn't inexpensive. My friends helped, I had some savings, and my boyfriend contributed. I never told my parents. Afterward, I was so relieved. Those are the only words I have for it: deeply relieved. It was what I wanted, and I made it happen. I went on with my life.

You might disagree with my choice, and you might think this has nothing to do with finance. But actually, it has everything to do with what

INTRODUCTION

I want to teach you in this book. These days, I know that people see me as this successful woman with a great career, great family, and access to wealth. But while I grew up in a good family, I'm very aware that my life could easily have gone another direction.

For me, financial independence has meant being able to live my life according to my own volition. It meant being in a position where, if things didn't go my way, or if my father was hitting me with his belt, I could leave. And I did leave: I went away to college, and I never looked back.

Today, as a financial professional, I regularly meet women who are hesitant to commit to financial goals and uncomfortable advocating for themselves around money. That discomfort matters. A 25-year-old woman who starts out making the same amount as her male colleague might gradually make less due to lower raises or smaller bonuses. She eventually becomes a 50-year-old woman who has made significantly less than she might have over her lifetime.

Even today, the truth is that men still ask for more, and they ask more often. Plus, let's be honest: they're not typically the person in the family who steps back from a career to take care of children or aging parents; likewise, they're not usually the one who steps back when a spouse's career accelerates. They have maximum time and maximum opportunities to earn.

Every woman has a moment when she realizes the importance of having agency to move toward something she wants or away from something that's hurting her. That moment may not be as dramatic as avoiding corporal punishment or ending an accidental pregnancy, but I'm sure there has been a moment in your life where you've needed to escape or wanted to dream bigger. This book is about how money can help you do that—how women *must* use money *in order* to do that. I know that it was a path to freedom for me. And it's one that anyone can find.

* * *

Much of the financial inequality women still experience today is driven by fear. Women are savvier about money today than we've ever been, taking control and building knowledge and wealth. But there's a long way to go and anxiety to overcome. The earlier we begin, the better.

One way to seize more control is to start by talking more about all of this—and explicitly from a female perspective. That's why this book is called *It's Time to Talk*. It's one part handbook for personal money *management*, one part guide to money *communication*, or all the talking about our finances we need to do with important people in our lives. Many of our financial difficulties are really about how money makes us feel or how it affects our relationships. We may be afraid of facing our own shame and insecurity. We may want to have a money conversation with someone but haven't because we don't know how to start.

All this is understandable! Many people, maybe even most people, shrink from discussions about money. (I know because they tell me constantly, "I don't like to talk about money.") Just consider the words we use in those conversations we do have: they're emotional, not rational. "You're wasteful," or "You're spending too much," or "You don't have enough." So much judgment! I can't tell you how often I hear, "I should know this, I feel so ashamed."

Let's take the shame out of it. Think about the difference it could make in your life to have those conversations now, the sense of relief and empowerment you would feel if you stopped putting them off. This book will give you clarity on your own finances, showing you the way to the path you want, and getting you started walking down it. Then it will support you in the conversations you need to have along the way.

For example, do you dread talking to your spouse about money? Maybe your partner is the one who keeps track of all things financial and you don't want to rock the boat. Maybe your eyes glaze over when you talk about money, but you'd like to master the details and feel more confident. We'll talk about how to set up Money Dates, a low-pressure and specific time to get together and talk about mutually shared money matters—then enjoy a slice of cake or a hike together.

Maybe you need to talk with your parents about their financial situation. They're retired, and you're unsure how they've prepared for this next chapter of their lives, or you need their help financially but you grew up in a family that avoided discussing money at all costs. I'll help you create a framework for setting up that conversation with boundaries that will help everyone in the conversation be comfortable.

Or perhaps you're thinking about getting divorced, but you have no idea where to start. I'll take you through the process of safeguarding yourself financially before you tell anyone else—and definitely before you take your first steps.

I want all of us to feel at ease talking about money. Controlling your own pot of money is essential if you want to leave a relationship that is no longer working for you (whether it's with a parent, a boss, a city, or a partner). It will allow you to take a dream job in a new town or to pay for an education that will give you a leg up. It will allow you to make the choices that are best for you and those who rely on you. But it also means you must accept your role as boss of your own financial life and embrace the interpersonal challenges that come with that position. Once you're comfortable, you will be able to have the conversations you need to have with your partner, your parents, your boss, and the people in your life that need you.

Many great money guides on the market are aimed at new college graduates or soon-to-be retirees. They're important and helpful. But many of these guides don't address the "why" and "how" of issues that are specific to women. They don't address the cultural taboo of talking about money, which keeps us from understanding how to make it work for us. They don't account for our stepping out of the workforce to raise children or care for aging family members. They ignore that women tend to live longer and often outlive their spouses. And they overlook that because women aren't

Introduction

paid equally over the course of our working lives, the proportion of us who live in poverty in retirement is substantially higher.

Learning about money is the first step to countering these dire statistics. It may all feel a bit unfamiliar at first. But resolving that discomfort really comes down to practice: pushing through your comfort zone and understanding there's no downside to learning more. If it's new territory, the more comfortable you are being uncomfortable, the more quickly you'll learn.

My tax-paying life has taken me from McDonald's to executive roles with Wall Street firms to work as a financial advisor, focusing on new business and helping my clients navigate their financial lives. I want to share these conversations with you (though of course I've changed all names and identifying characteristics to maintain confidentiality). I've been in many of the difficult positions you have, and no one was there to walk me through them. I did find it overwhelming sometimes to make my own way. But I worked it out—and you can too. I hope that in sharing what I learned from my mistakes, I'll be able to help you avoid yours.

* * *

So, how did I put my family issues and high school challenges behind me, move from my childhood in Indiana, and eventually become the author of this book? My plan was to go to college, join the Foreign Service, and travel the world. I studied in Japan during my junior year of college. There, for the first time, I met Ivy League kids whose parents (typically their fathers) worked in top financial firms. Many of my friends planned to do that too. I didn't really understand yet what that meant, but the prospect of financial success appealed to me enough to reconsider the idea of becoming a junior diplomat.

To start in this new direction, I had to get to New York. My first job out of college was at a large insurance company with an office in lower Manhattan. While it was a pretty terrific entry-level job, I had set my sights on Wall Street. I befriended people with entry-level finance jobs, who explained the role of salesperson, trader, and analyst. They introduced me to their seniors and to HR departments. I interviewed with many companies and eventually landed my first job in finance.

But financial markets are cyclical. It's not unusual during a market downturn to suddenly lose your job. You walk in one morning and walk out with a box of your belongings before noon.

The first time I was laid off, I was blindsided by what were called "market forces." It had never occurred to me that I could lose my job. I was paid well and was contributing to a 401(k) retirement plan each month through my employer, but I didn't have much extra savings. Living in New York was expensive: I had to worry about rent, student loan payments, utility bills, and groceries. My unemployment and severance didn't go very far.

An emergency fund would have been helpful. Unfortunately, I didn't have one. No one had ever explained the importance of emergency savings. I knew I should pay my bills on time and not buy things I couldn't afford. I understood that I needed to save and thought I was doing a good job because I was contributing to my 401(k) plan. Having a separate emergency fund had never crossed my mind.

In the end, I had to liquidate my meager 401(k) funds to pay my rent. While it was a comparatively small amount, it had taken me five years to save and grow those funds. Plus, I had to pay a penalty for early withdrawal and taxes on the gains. I still remember it as one of my biggest money mistakes but also one of my most valuable money lessons. Instead of holding onto my retirement nest egg, I had to start again at zero. (Lesson 1: Maintain a separate emergency fund in a money market, high-yield savings, or CD account for easy access. Think of a 401(k) only as money that is "off limits" until you're retired.)

I hit the job market hard and was hired by a new firm. I never wanted to find myself in that fearful position again, and I set about educating myself. For the first time, I came to understand the difference between

Introduction

institutional finance, which I was learning about at work, and personal finance. This was pre-internet, so I read books, took classes, and scanned personal finance magazines. Slowly, carefully, I invested and became my friends' go-to person for personal financial advice.

A couple of years later, during another market correction, my firm downsized my department. This time, I had a reasonable emergency fund, which gave me some peace of mind. I ended up spending that summer in a beach house I rented with friends, training for my first marathon. It was one of the best summers of my life, and I found a new job and returned to work that fall.

* * *

Since then, I've had a good run in finance, but there have been lean years. At times, I've had to be frugal. Every industry experiences ups and downs. When my kids were young, we shared hand-me-downs with friends and happily traded gently used toys at the neighborhood swap meet. Now that I work with individuals and families, I emphasize that we all make choices about how to spend money. Even Bill Gates can't fund everything he wants to fund.

I use the word "choice" intentionally. I could have said that everyone makes "sacrifices," but framing these decisions as choices emphasizes the strength of the person choosing. As we begin to discuss financial empowerment—your financial empowerment—let's focus on framing, learning to think differently. "I'm making a choice to save here; I'm making a choice to spend there," means *all this* is within your power. Part of claiming this control means you may need to learn to think and communicate differently.

Even today, women routinely suffer financially from speaking up about poor treatment. They can and do lose their jobs or get passed over for the next promotion because of often legitimate complaints. But what if the woman speaking out against a substandard boss was in a financial position that gave her confidence to respond to undeserved treatment? What if she could feel absolutely comfortable asking for a raise or promotion, knowing how to link her performance to financial reward? What if she could feel comfortable speaking up against sexist jokes and behavior or providing feedback to a patronizing manager? She could feel secure saying, "This isn't right," knowing that she and her family wouldn't suffer.

When I was on Wall Street, everyone talked about "F—You Money." That's money that allows you to make decisions based entirely on what you do—or do not—want to do.

I want to teach you how to manage your money, how to use it to enhance your own power, and how to communicate effectively about it. And I want you to believe you can be a fully realized woman who is able to navigate financial relationships with authenticity, ask for what she deserves, and take care of herself and the people who need her. That is *absolutely* within your reach. Let's get started.

PART I

MONEY TALKS: BUILDING YOUR FINANCIAL FLUENCY

CHAPTER ONE

MASTERING THE BASICS: CREDIT, SAVINGS, AND AN EMERGENCY FUND

I've noticed certain patterns among the couples I've worked with in my years as a financial professional. In every relationship, someone does more laundry, someone does more cooking, someone does more of the shopping. That happens with money too: one person often takes more responsibility for bills and money management.

Very seldom have I seen a couple in which each party is equally engaged with their personal finances. Sometimes, one person focuses on making money, while the other keeps a budgeting spreadsheet. One person takes the time to learn about new investment opportunities, while the other keeps track of bills. That sharing of labor is a good practice. But it's vital that both partners are involved in *financial planning*. If you don't know how to cook, and the person who cooks leaves you, you can probably figure out how to get fed. If you don't know how to do laundry, it's not that hard—you can figure out how to wash your clothes. But what happens when we're talking about money?

Darla, a woman I met recently, had been married for a long time when her husband took her out to dinner and asked for a divorce. She was caught unawares; the idea of divorce had not been on her radar at all. She, a well-educated woman, had chosen to stay home with their kids, and was not particularly engaged with the family finances, so you can imagine her fear. Darla's mind was flooded with anxious questions: What does this mean for me? Will I have to sell the house? I've been out of the workforce for 10 years; will it be hard for me to return? What's my retirement savings plan now? Will I qualify for alimony? How does child support work? All these questions accompanied the devastating realizations that her spouse was leaving, and she was going to spend less time with her beloved children.

In a similar vein, I've been working recently with Reina, a client whose husband died unexpectedly. It was a big shock. Together, they were paying the mortgage; together, they'd been working toward their financial goals. And then, suddenly, he was gone, and Reina was left to sort out not just her life without him but also her financial situation. She had been engaged financially, but he had done most of the active work. The proceeds from his life insurance were meager. Figuring out how to stay in her home was challenging.

And then there's my acquaintance, Li. Smart and well educated, with a good job, Li never really engaged with her money, and she never married, so no one shouldered that responsibility with her. Although she has some savings, she doesn't have a big-picture plan and has never invested. As we've grown older, I've started to worry for her. How is she going to retire? (People often say, "I'm never going to retire. I'm going to work till I die." That may be what they want to do, but often it's out of their control.)

These women weren't ever taught how to think about money. Their parents or teachers or employers never explained IRAs; no one taught them how to save for retirement. That's not their fault, and it's nothing to be ashamed of. And if that's true of you, it's not your fault, either. But whether you are 16 and just starting your work life, or 60 and contemplating retirement, now is the time to take interest. Being complacent about your finances has consequences sooner or later.

Women like Darla and Reina find themselves navigating situations they never expected or realizing after decades of work that they've been victims of a chronic gender pay gap. Not being paid what you're worth when you're working will impact the amount of money you can set aside in your Individual Retirement Account (IRA), your 401(k) plan, various investment accounts, and the quality of the home you can buy. It all adds up (or doesn't) over time, and the results can be disastrous.

To stop that from happening, to claim control, you must first understand all this stuff. Once you understand it, you can wield it; once you can wield it, you can talk about it; once you talk about it, you can banish that fear.

It's never too late to start. In order to have the conversations around money that are central to the latter part of this book, you first need to get in control of your financial future now. And in order to do that, you need to understand its various facets: Saving, Budgeting, Planning for Retirement, Investment, Managing Debt, and Contributing to Charity. Let's begin.

WHAT'S A CREDIT SCORE?

Before you buy your first car, before you graduate from college, before you start your first job, you can begin to lay the groundwork for a positive financial future. It all starts with a credit score.

A credit score is a way for banks, companies, or lenders to understand how creditworthy you are—that is, how likely you are to pay them back if they give you a loan. Your credit score impacts a huge swath of your life, from renting your first apartment to helping your kids get loans for college and setting your mortgage rate, car loan, and credit card interest rates. (Disparities in interest rates you're offered might seem small, but over time the difference is considerable. Say you're paying 4%, and I'm paying 5% for the same loan. That means I'm paying 25% more than you are, which is a big difference when we're talking about hundreds or thousands of dollars. For example, the total interest paid over the life of a 30-year mortgage at 4% versus 5% for a $300,000 loan is almost $65,000.) Some companies even look at your score as part of your background check before they hire you.

Credit scores range from a low of 300 to a high of 850, and a credit score of 720 or higher is considered very good. Several factors affect your credit score, including the length of your credit history (how long you've had and used credit), your payment history (do you pay your bills on time or are you chronically late?), current and past debts, types of credit in use, and recently opened accounts.

You can start to build your credit score as early as high school or college: a credit card in your name is one way to start, if your parents are willing to help you get it. A student loan is also another way to build a credit score, as long as you pay it consistently every month.

> You're legally allowed to see your credit score at least once every year for free through three American credit agencies: TransUnion, Equifax, and Experian. The Annual Credit Report website makes it simple, or you can request scores directly from the agencies themselves. The record they pull for you will reflect how many times you've applied for credit, your payment history, any history of late payments, what your maximum available credit is, and how much debt you have outstanding. It's all online and easy to track.

Don't take the freedom (and responsibility) of having credit in your own name for granted. For a long time, women could not get credit cards or own property in their own names. That changed with the 1974 Equal Credit Opportunity Act. (Yes, you read that right, barely 50 years ago.) If you're a single woman and want to buy a house, and you don't want to pay more for it than the guy you sit next to at work, understanding how to manage your credit cards and score matters. If you're an entrepreneur and you need a bank loan, a good credit score can boost your chances of getting the best rate.

A good credit score enables you to access money to do the things you want to do: go to graduate school, buy a house or a car, travel to Asia, or make a life change when you want to.

HOW SHOULD I USE MY CREDIT CARDS?

When I was in my twenties and living on my own in New York, I had at least 10 credit cards. I clearly hadn't learned about credit scores! I had my Bloomingdales card for my clothes shopping, my Smith and Wollensky card for the nights when I wanted a nice steak dinner. No one told me, "You know, that's a lot to keep track of. You could easily lose control of your spending this way, and it could negatively affect your credit score."

I figured that out eventually, through trial and error, and that's how I ended up with a few golden rules for credit cards:

1. Only keep two credit cards at any one time.
   Use one as your primary card, and one as a backup. Most of us don't need more than that. Avoid department store credit cards, although I know they can be tempting. They're all about getting the brand in front of you and encouraging you to spend your money there. Instead, do your research on the benefits of each of your two

non-department store cards, and figure out which are the best for you. Do you do a lot of flying? Go with a card that offers miles as a reward. Do you get a boost when you get cash back on your purchases? Go find that.

If you already have a bunch of extra credit cards, don't cancel them all at once because that can hurt your credit score too. Instead, just stop using them, or freeze the accounts and put them away. And yes, I mean *freeze*. I literally advise putting credit cards you aren't using in a plastic bag, adding water, and freezing them. Then, if you really want to use them, they are easy to access, and you will have time to think about your spending plan while they defrost.

2. Pay off your credit card balance every month.

    Credit cards interest rates are wildly high, and each month you don't pay off your balance, interest will accrue and the total amount due will grow substantially. It's easier to keep track of everything when you only have two cards to pay off.

3. Don't max out your credit line every month.

    This one is a rule many people don't know about, including people who are generally informed about responsible credit card use. Regularly maxing out your credit line, even if you're good about paying it off, will negatively affect your credit score. So, if you have a $10,000 credit limit, don't spend $9,500. Instead, think $3,000 or less. Keeping your spending or credit utilization ratio below 30% of your credit limit is ideal. (But not spending at all can also backfire, since that can affect your credit score. It's good to use your emergency card[s] once in a while and pay any bills off promptly.) If you find yourself bumping up against your limit often, call your credit card company and ask about increasing your credit line. If you've been reliable about paying every month and can back it up with a pay stub that shows you are being paid a salary that can support an increased limit, they are likely to say yes.

Mastering the Basics: Credit, Savings, and an Emergency Fund

WHAT IS AN EMERGENCY FUND?

As I learned the hard way, building up an emergency fund is a first step in financial independence. This is money you have set aside in advance to pay for unexpected and urgent expenses. Those expenses could come from losing your job, getting sick, or having your car break down. To figure out how much you should set aside, calculate your after-tax income or total your expenses for a given month, then multiply that number by at least 3 and anywhere up to 12.

This might sound too obvious, too simple, but the fact is that many Americans can't or don't set emergency savings aside. According to the 2024 Bankrate Emergency Savings Survey, 27% of all Americans have no emergency fund, and 59% of Americans can't put their hands on $1,000 in case of emergency. Yet the average emergency room visit ranges from $1,500 to $3,000 without insurance. Nearly everyone faces an unexpected event each year—so it behooves us to plan for it. If you don't have to tap your fund this year, you can rest assured you will have that money set aside when something urgent does come up—because eventually it will.

How much is enough? Let's do some more math here. In the fourth quarter of 2023, the median weekly salary for American women was $1,031. That equals about $4,500 per month, or about $54,000 a year. Depending on where you live, your state and city tax will be different, but let's use an example of a single woman living in San Francisco, California. After tax, her net pay would be approximately $3,551 per month. Thus, as a minimum emergency fund, she would want to build up to at least $10,653 in savings.

Still, the average only gets us so far here. This is about what is best for you specifically. If you are a hotshot tech employee and know you could walk out of your current job to one right next door (and for equal or greater pay), then an emergency fund of three months is probably adequate. If you are older, a person of color, a senior in your field, or working in an industry that can be cyclical or that is overstaffed, then it may make sense to have more like 6–12 months' salary saved up, because it could take you longer to find a new job. As we learned in early 2025, even government jobs aren't secure; having access to ample emergency funds is important for everyone.

Regardless of your personal profile or your profession, everyone is vulnerable to a car accident or a broken leg. But an emergency fund is especially important for women because, with their average lower earnings, women are generally able to save less. Gender also makes a difference when it comes to social protections like unemployment. Women are less likely to qualify for unemployment, and if they do qualify, it is often for much less than they expected. That's because they're more likely to have stayed briefly in jobs, to have been paid under the table, or to have been paid less than their male coworkers.

The average woman's Social Security payout is also substantially lower. According to the Social Security Administration, in December 2023, the average annual woman's Social Security income was $20,562.24, compared to $25,276.80 for the average man. That was in part because women take more breaks to care for children or other family members. This is not particularly fair, but until we elect politicians who will advocate to change that, it's up to us to make sure we're protected in case of an emergency.

WHAT'S AN IRA?

The letters stand for "Individual Retirement Account." An IRA is money put aside for retirement, invested with a reputable brokerage in a way that makes sense for your stage of life, is aligned with your values, and takes into account your capacity for risk and volatility. You pay taxes on the money you put in a regular IRA in the future, when you take the money out. The Internal Revenue Service sets a universal maximum everyone can put into an IRA each year; in 2025, that number was $7,000. If you are 50 and older, a "catch-up" provision allows you to put in $1,000 more.

A regular IRA is different from a Roth IRA. That's a specific type of IRA that has salary limits. (These limits and caps also change periodically, so they need to be confirmed each year.) You put money in a Roth IRA *after* you've paid taxes. Then, when you take your money out at a future date, it comes out tax free. You can have both kinds of IRAs over your lifetime, and there are benefits to both, but you can only contribute to one at a time.

Then there's a Spousal IRA, a type of account people don't talk about enough. Let's say you're married, and your husband works but you don't. He's putting money in his IRA, but since you're not working, you might think you don't qualify for an IRA yourself. Not true; you can open a Spousal IRA if you file a joint tax return with your working spouse. You can put the same amount that your spouse contributes into your own account to build up your retirement savings.

If you are just learning about IRAs, don't stress; it's better to start late than never. IRAs are especially important to your financial well-being as a woman. We drop out of the workforce for all kinds of reasons, including caring for children and elderly family members. Those pauses can mean that women aren't employed at workplaces long enough to qualify and participate in their company's 401(k) plans—we'll get to those in a minute—or they work in jobs that don't offer a 401(k) plan.

Because they're available to anyone earning money and paying taxes, IRAs are an essential alternative for retirement savings if you don't work for a company that offers a 401(k) plan. They are doubly important for nonworking spouses. The annual amount might not seem like a lot at first, but the earlier you start saving and the longer you keep at it, the more it will add up over time. Also, note that an IRA is something you can have *in addition* to putting money in a 401(k) plan. You can do both, but it's important to understand the limits of each type of plan and speak with a tax professional or financial advisor to get the correct accounts for you.

WHAT'S THE DIFFERENCE BETWEEN AN IRA AND A 401(K)?

A 401(k) is the most common company-sponsored investment plan offered as a benefit to employees for the purpose of retirement savings. (If you work for a nonprofit, you might have something similar, like a 403(b).) Whereas an IRA is something that's yours—you start it, you fund it, you control it—a 401(k) is company controlled. You put in funds pretax from earned income, and that money grows "tax deferred," meaning you don't pay taxes on it until you take it out. That means your tax load is reduced each year you contribute to your retirement plan. Many companies will match a percentage of the funds you put in, which is a great perk.

Later, if you leave your job, your 401(k) funds are portable. You can often roll them into your next employer's 401(k) or into your IRA. The portability of a 401(k) means that whatever money you put in is yours; however, the matching percentage your company offers often "vests" over a certain period. This means you have to work at a company for a specific period (the "vesting period") before you can fully own the amount that company contributed. If you are thinking of leaving your company, be sure to check when your 401(k) match becomes yours. You wouldn't want to miss taking the match with you if you don't have to.

The rise of the 401(k) can be traced to the decline of pension plans. Until the 1970s, pensions were a standard employee benefit. But over the last 50 years, it has become increasingly expensive for companies to fund pensions for employees and to maintain investment teams to manage that money. Increasingly, corporate America hasn't wanted to take on or maintain that burden, so retirement savings went from an employ*er* responsibility to an employ*ee* responsibility. That's a loss for employees for many reasons, particularly because the burden is now on employees to manage that money, and most of us don't have the interest or skillset to do it. (We'll talk more about this later in the book.)

Although your company controls your 401(k), you usually have some input into how the money in your account gets invested. Most companies have a menu of investment options to choose from. Unfortunately, companies often offer minimal advice on which options to choose, often relying on HR professionals instead of investment professionals. In general, it's a good idea to aim for a well-balanced portfolio that reflects your overall financial goals and is neither too aggressive nor too conservative. We'll get more into investment strategy later too.

Some firms have automatic enrollment, meaning they take a certain amount of your paycheck each pay period and put it in your 401(k) retirement account without you having to do anything. It's usually anywhere from 3% to 5%, because that is the percentage most companies match. More often, you'll need to enroll yourself; in that case, don't put it off. It's essential that you take advantage of one of the key benefits your company offers to help you build wealth.

Once you enroll, you can contribute up to a total of $23,500 a year if you're under 50 years old, not counting what your company offers. Once you're over age 50, the maximum increases. (The previous number reflects 2025, but these amounts change periodically too.) A 401(k) is for most people the number one way to build tax-deferred wealth for retirement. Since women tend to live longer, educating ourselves about how to manage ours is crucial to our well-being in old age. If you get divorced, your 401(k) and IRA become a reliable pot of money for supporting yourself. (Note, though, that retirement funds are often part of divorce settlements—meaning that in some circumstances when you separate, they may need to be divided between you and your spouse.)

If you're a gig worker, an independent contractor, or a self-employed owner of a business, you might think you don't have access to a 401(k). But you're in luck, you have options! As the owner of a business with no employees, you can open a solo, or single participant, 401(k). And since you're technically both the employer and the employee, you can contribute more to that account. Consult a tax or financial professional to discuss details.

HOW MUCH SAVINGS IS ENOUGH FOR RETIREMENT?

This is a common question, and my response is always: "It depends." The answer is different for everyone. The many retirement calculators out there can help you figure out what "enough" is, but you also need to take time to actually *think* about how much you're going to need. Fidelity Investments, for example, has an age-based approach that works well, since knowing how much you need to save by a given age will help you stay on track and reach your goals. By age 30, they suggest you should have the equivalent of 50% of your annual salary in accumulated savings. If you're 40, you want to have saved twice your annual salary. If you're 50, you want to have four times your salary in the bank. And if you're pushing 60, you want six times your annual salary saved. This is also assuming that you have this money invested in a manner that will grow. For most people, I advise that their retirement savings *not* be kept in a savings account with very low returns.

Another popular formula to find the right savings target, known as the Bengen Rule, suggests you should divide your desired annual retirement income by 0.04, as 4% has proven over time to be a reasonable annual distribution rate on invested assets. Let's say you want $100,000 a year in retirement. Then your aim should be to save $2.5 million, since $100,000/0.04 = $2,500,000. While the Bengen Rule has been updated at least a few times, suffice it to say that if your withdrawal rate is equal to your earnings, your portfolio should maintain itself over time.

A note about Social Security: I know Social Security is part of most people's retirement planning. I have a cousin who lives in a state where the cost of living is lower, and her Social Security benefits cover many of her expenses. But in many parts of the United States, Social Security alone may not be enough to maintain your quality of life. If Social Security is a big part of your current retirement plans, I encourage you to go to the Social Security Administration website and look up how much you'll be receiving. Anyone can do it, and knowing your expected payout will help you plan. The difficult fact is that for most people, it won't be enough, and I want you to be able to change course if you need to.

GETTING STARTED

Here are some first steps to get you started and create momentum:

1. The first step is understanding your options. Ask someone at work tomorrow (probably someone in HR) if your employer offers a 401(k) plan and if you're qualified to enroll. If you are, consider enrolling immediately.
2. Then, if you don't already have an IRA, go online to Schwab, Fidelity, or Vanguard to learn about the IRAs, Roth IRAs, and Spousal IRAs they offer and the fund choices that are available. There's so much great information online, and these institutions are a great place to start.

3. When it comes to saving, my mantra is: "always pay yourself first." Pull out a piece of paper and figure out how much you can save every month. If you have zero idea where to start, that's fine. The general rule of thumb, based on lots of deep academic research, is to put away 15–20% of your gross income (that's before deductions and taxes) each pay period. If you begin with your very first paychecks, you'll get in the habit of putting away that amount and won't even miss it. Focus first on saving three months' worth of pay for your emergency fund, plus making contributions to your 401(k)—at least to the amount your company is matching—or IRA.
4. It might take some time for that to be possible. Don't be hard on yourself if that's the case. Ask yourself what feels like a doable amount as a starting point and begin there; maybe 10% feels more reachable. Really, any amount is a good start, whether it's $10 or $100. Put half in your emergency fund savings account and the other half in your retirement account and repeat every pay period. Set up your accounts so the money comes right out of your paycheck and goes directly to your bank. We'll talk more about this in the next chapter.
5. As you do all that, you might consider joining an investment club to learn more, as well. Or you might open another nonretirement account and learn about index funds. Follow your nose based on what feels interesting and exciting to you. (Note that if you invest at an institution like Fidelity or Schwab, you can take advantage of their advisors to analyze your financial needs and set up a retirement plan at the same time.)

Reina's story shows the power of even these simple actions. I'm happy to say that after her crisis, things have worked out well for her. She sold her home and bought a new one in a more affordable, up-and-coming neighborhood. She decided she could allocate more of her salary to her retirement savings plan. We had candid conversations about her new dreams for herself and her children, we assessed her assets and her debts, and we calculated how many years she needs to keep working. Then we set up an emergency fund as well as a fun fund. What started out as a tragic and traumatic event is still emotionally hard, but now she's on solid financial ground. She would be the first to tell you that she knew very little about her family's finances before, yet she has managed to create a fabulous new life for herself.

You can do that too. Once you've covered the basics, you're free to think about your next investment goal. Would you like to buy a home, invest in stocks, follow your dream to go back to school, or take out loans to start a business of your own?

As with everything else in your financial life, it will be a journey of discovery—one full of risks and rewards and that you'll feel ready for when the time is right. Learning to manage your money allows you to dream, and that can be exciting and a source of confidence rather than one of stress.

There are many people out there who can help you learn what you need to know—human resources departments that offer classes on 401(k)s, books like this, podcasts, or local community colleges. Many investment companies offer resources, such as investment advisors who are willing to spend time with potential clients. And once you have a nest egg started, financial professionals like me will help you grow it for the long term.

I know I have thrown a lot of information your way in this first chapter. I'd suggest putting this book down for a moment, standing up, and stretching. Be patient with yourself. Learning and practicing enough to feel comfortable even with the basics of personal finance takes time. Don't expect to understand all this right away.

CHAPTER TWO

DREAMING BIG: A FUTURE THAT INSPIRES YOU

When I was a teenager, I knew I wanted to live in a city. I didn't have a lot of specifics in mind, but I knew I wanted to live by myself, do interesting work, wear great clothes, and travel.

When I graduated from college, I was fortunate to land a good entry-level job that moved me to New York City. A few years later, I found an even better job, one that paid me well enough that I could buy some of those great clothes. It was an international role; when I wasn't traveling for work, I traveled for fun as much as possible.

Then, at some point in my mid-thirties, I realized I did want to get married and have kids, so I started focusing on making that happen. I've always felt strongly that it's important to imagine and honor what you want. Once you can see your goals, figure out a plan and take steps toward them.

So far, I'm not saying anything out of the ordinary. But while I realize that life often surprises us and that obstacles can be placed before us, we're rarely encouraged to connect our big-picture dreams with hard numbers. In this chapter, you'll let your imagination run free so that you can plot the bigger-picture steps to move toward your goals. In the next chapter, we'll analyze the specific numbers you need to make it happen. And then in Part Two of the book, we'll go through the money conversations you'll have with the people around you along the way.

START DREAMING

Moving from focusing on what you want to clear numbers that will help you get there is like training for a marathon. First, you set your goal, then work backward, calculating the steps you can do today (and the next day, and the day after that) to achieve that goal. It's a simple math problem combined with a vision board, and what you get at the end is a *findable number*. Here's how you find it.

Block off some time, pull out a big piece of paper (we can call it your Dreams Paper), and start daydreaming. What's on your bucket list? What do you want your life to feel like? What kind of community do you want to live in? What do you want your life to look like 5 years from now, 10 years from now? Write down everything you want, really, everything you can think of. Draw pictures, add photos. No goal or dream is too small or too big, too nitty-gritty or too outlandish. This is for you, not for anybody else.

Don't worry about overcommitting. When I consider my New Year's intentions, I understand I'm not going to prioritize all of them. But by putting it all on paper, I've planted an important seed for myself about the direction I want to go. When you write it down and start to visualize it, you will begin to move in that direction. And if you can start to understand the path to those intentions, then you can start envisioning what kind of financial life you need to achieve that dream.

WEIGH THE SCENIC ROUTE VERSUS THE EXPRESS TRAIN

I mean this in two different ways. One is about how soon you want to achieve the goals you've set. The other is how ambitious, from a cost perspective, those goals may be.

Let's say you want to travel for six months. If you save aggressively for a year or two then quit your job, maybe you could travel on a tight budget for six months. Or you could choose to work for a few more years, saving at a more leisurely pace, and then take a more luxurious six-month trip.

If it's your priority to get there sooner rather than later, maybe you're willing to make a lot of sacrifices on a daily basis. Alternatively, though, you may think: "It could be tough to live so frugally for three years. Instead, I can take a slower path while prioritizing saving and accept it may take me seven years to get there." Great! Make that choice.

This question also applies to how you want your route to look in a more philosophical sense. Think about your values. What's important to you? How are your values reflected in your financial choices? Are you a "carpe diem" person or a planner? Are you a lover of luxury or a more pragmatic type who likes the simple and functional?

Start asking what *you* care about—not what anyone else says you should, nor what society deems important. What motivates you? If it thrills you to wear designer clothes, you can build a life that allows you to do that. Some people are happy to drive the same car for 10 years but splash out on an expensive refrigerator—because they spend a lot of time in the kitchen and having top-notch appliances brings them joy. Some people forgo the car altogether and take the bus, putting their money toward a long trip each year. Honestly, the "what" of it doesn't matter. Our time on this planet is finite. Figure out how you want to live here and use the skills you'll gain in this book to think about how you're going to make the numbers support the life you want.

FACE YOUR FEARS

The flipside of letting yourself dream big is truly a flipside. Financial planning isn't just about the highest highs. It's also about the lowest lows, planning for the worst possibility. That means spending some time considering your deepest fears. For example, "bag lady syndrome" plagues many women—the fear of losing everything and ending up on the street.

While I'm not a psychologist, I find that if I don't acknowledge my fears, I leave space for them to come true, leading myself right down a path toward them. You might be so worried about becoming homeless that you become paralyzed, thinking, "I don't want to look at my bank account; I don't want to know how close I am to having nothing." Then you spend blindly.

So, on the other side of your Dreams Paper, explore some of your fears. What are you afraid of? What do you envision when someone says, "What's the worst that could happen?" Underneath each fear, have a conversation with yourself. What actions are you taking that could lead you down this path? Are you creating extra debt for yourself? Are you working in a job that is underpaying you, and are there alternatives to that job you're not acknowledging? Are you not saving, or not investing, enough money? Then, answer yourself: What kind of systems might you put in place to shore things up and achieve success? Remember, taking control of your finances is the most effective way to ensure that the worst-case scenario will not come true. In fact, taking control of our financial lives will help eliminate anxiety-based procrastination. Action has the power to dissipate fear.

IMAGINE THE WORK YOU WANT

Why do we work? Have you ever asked yourself that question—and I mean really asked yourself?

For much of my early career, I worked on a trading floor on an institutional sales desk. I felt as though I was standing at the center of the global heartbeat. My colleagues were smart people who synthesized economic and political news and considered how it would impact the portfolios of the money managers we worked with every day. It was intellectually stimulating and high stress. (Stress is not always a bad thing.) We believed we were making a difference.

Today, my work still brings me a deep sense of satisfaction: In addition to helping families build, protect, and grow their wealth, we often discuss how they can pass a sense of service on to their children and how they take care of their friends or community. It is deeply fulfilling to know that my colleagues and I can help *them* make a difference.

Work does not have to be, and hopefully isn't, only about making money and survival. Even modest work can be fulfilling. It provides a place to go each day and an essential structure, as well as the satisfactions of collaboration. We like tackling new projects and feel significant when we do a good job. We (hopefully) like and respect our coworkers. It feels good to grow in a job and to know that our contribution matters to the success of our organizations.

Knowing what kind of work you want to do is paramount—whether you're just graduating from college or considering a career pivot. Some workplaces are warmer, more inclusive environments, others deeply competitive. Some are very mission-driven, others more profit-motivated. Start with some brainstorming. Reflect on your level of professional ambition and your desire for work-life balance.

On a new Dreams Paper, make a list of what kind of tasks get you excited. What have you enjoyed doing in the past? What do you want your life to look like in 3, 5, and 10 years? Do you enjoy an intense workplace? Do you like a structured office environment? Do you want to work in a big city? Do you prefer a small office with a group of close-knit colleagues or a large and cosmopolitan one?

This brainstorming could also include informational interviews: turn to your network to teach you what you could be doing. Since I make a list for everything, I'd recommend making one of everyone you know who does something you think is interesting. Don't be shy about including friends of your parents or extended family, friends of friends, etc. (People often think a network has to be some fancy thing. Even if it's not through your family, I'm sure you know someone you could ask for help.) My husband and I spend a lot of time talking to other people's kids, and we appreciate it when our friends do the same for ours; that's what community is about. And always finish your conversation with a thank-you and by asking: "Is there anyone else you think I should talk to?"

Whether you're freshly graduated or changing jobs, you might not have a passion for the most lucrative job offer you receive. Do you hold out and keep looking or take the job offered? I always tell the people I mentor: Who knows where this opportunity will lead? A job should appeal to you, but there are no perfect jobs. Stay flexible. Maybe you'll start out in a marketing job and realize that you'd actually prefer working in the chief financial officer (CFO) office because finance turns you on. Or you planned to go to law school, then realize that engineering is your passion.

You may have never deeply explored how you work before, even if you're well into your career, but it's not too late to start. You don't have to (and are unlikely to!) stay forever, but every job offers lessons. Even if you hate it, you're going to learn something, and it might be more interesting than you think. Plus, it's always easier to get a new job when you have a job.

DON'T FORGET ABOUT THE MONEY

In an ideal world, all these questions about values, fulfillment, purpose would be where you'd start any conversation about work. That's often where women *do* go first in these conversations. But other stuff also matters. We often hear that the salary shouldn't matter, but that's a pretty privileged position to start from, and it can be a damaging assumption. On the other side of my "why do we work" question lie the practicalities. One reason we work is for the money, and that in turn enables us to financially support ourselves and our families.

Given all this focus on values, when I talk with young women about their goals, they often tell me, "I'd love to work for a nonprofit and change the world." They're not considering how they're going to make rent while they're doing that. Joining a non-profit right out of school at a very junior level may align with your values, but it may not pay much. Meanwhile, are you actually contributing to that organization? Are you developing skills? Does the entry-level work make you feel fulfilled?

If you're willing to make the financial choices to make it work, you don't mind tightening your belt, and it fills your soul, kudos. But so often I see women take jobs that pay them less when they could have pursued more remunerative opportunities. Sometimes, they haven't stopped to consider what that choice means for their long-term financial wellness and their long-term personal fulfillment.

Your circumstances may influence your ability to make those choices. Maybe your cost of living is lower because of where you live or you are able to ask your parents for financial support. Maybe you're a person who's able to be very frugal. Maybe you plan to alternate between corporate and nonprofit jobs throughout your career. These factors may make it easier for you to prioritize your values and mission over salary. You may be happy living frugally with a tight budget. Your best friend may think carefully about her purchases but buys new items more often. What about you? If you make the choice to take lower pay, are you clear on the ramifications down the road?

If you take a low-paying job because you believe in the work, will you be able to save during that time? Will you be happy with your quality of life? How will you feel 10 years from now if this choice adds up to a dramatic difference in your savings? Will the limits imposed by your bank account bother you? Ask yourself these questions and answer them honestly.

Another option could include finding a corporate job that will give you a chance to develop the skills that nonprofits find valuable. If you spend a few years at the higher-paying job building your skills, résumé, and bank account, you create options for yourself. You'll have a couple of years of work experience and, hopefully, will have accumulated some savings. And you'll probably be even more valuable to that nonprofit because you will bring skills and training that will support their mission. They will likely be willing to pay you more in a higher value role. (If you're not sure about how to do this math, don't worry. We're going to get there in just a second.)

> If you're a solo entrepreneur or freelancer of any kind, a lot of your success will hinge on building relationships and a team, the professional contacts that you need to run your business successfully. Even if you're working *for* yourself, you're not usually working entirely *by* yourself. To determine what kind of legal and financial help you need, start by considering several questions:
>
> - How complex is the business you are running? Do you have any assistants or interns, or are you a solo practitioner?

- What are your business expenses, and how do you keep track of them?
- Do you have an insurance broker who helps you with insurance?
- Are you getting health insurance through your state's Affordable Care Act (ACA) marketplace? (Sometimes there are consultants paid by your state marketplace who can help figure out the plan that's right for you.)

First, you'll definitely need a good accountant and, ideally, a financial planner. (We'll talk more about these terms and how they differ later in the book.) How much money do you want to make; how much money do you need to make? What are the taxes and how do they work, when are they due? When and how much money do you need to set aside for taxes? If you're a freelancer filing self-employment taxes, it is almost always worthwhile to pay an accountant to help you with that. Taxes for freelancers are truly a pain in the butt, and chances are your accountant will know about deductions you can take that you would miss otherwise. Remember that you may be able to write off many different expenses on your taxes. It is very much in your interest to get educated about that.

Your money team will also be indispensable in helping you plan for retirement. A lot of people think that working for yourself puts you at a disadvantage for retirement planning, but there are real advantages to having your own business in terms of how much you can save every year. Start by looking into a SEP IRA or solo 401(k), or both. (Establishing a SEP IRA requires minimal paperwork and low administrative costs. You can do it even if you have employees. And since a solo 401(k) can have higher contribution limits per year for many people, that can do wonders for your savings down the road.)

It also doesn't hurt to have a business lawyer to review your legal documents and contracts. You don't need to have a lawyer on retainer, but you want to at least have the name of a lawyer to reach out to when you need advice. Then add the rest of your team: insurance brokers, health insurance and other consultants. You might consider establishing a relationship with a banker at your local bank who can be your point of contact as you grow your business. If you have relationships with other freelancers in your area and/or in your industry, they may be able to give you recommendations for people they work with.

IT'S TIME TO TALK

IMAGINE AND REIMAGINE

Regardless of the choices you make, remember that nothing is forever. "Imagining the work you want" is not a one-time process that only happens at the start of your professional life. The era when we had one job, one career trajectory to "set it and forget it" is gone, if it ever existed. Today, it's normal to go back to school to accelerate your career or to pivot to something new after stepping out a few years for childcare or to reinvent yourself after retirement.

One friend of mine had a successful career on Wall Street before she took 20 years off to raise her kids. A lot of Wall Street firms have very competitive "return to work" programs with thousands of applicants, and she was proud when she landed a spot at a large, nationally recognized brokerage firm. After a couple of years, she was doing very well and getting promoted—but she realized she really wanted to be working with individuals and families. So, she pivoted again, this time landing at a much smaller firm working as a wealth advisor, where she found her role much more fulfilling.

This kind of visioning can and should happen over and over, as we grow into our careers. There are some great books out there that will help you think more deeply about what pivots might be right for you. I particularly like *Working Identity* by Herminia Ibarra and *Getting Unstuck* by Timothy Butler as two starting points; you might also try *Switchers: How Smart Professionals Change Careers* by Dawn Graham or *Take the Leap: Change Your Career, Change Your Life* by Sara Bliss.

Maybe reading up on this topic sounds great, or maybe you'd rather not. Regardless, I would recommend scheduling some time at least once every year to reflect on some of these questions and how your answers may have changed. Are you doing what you want with your time? Is your work meeting your needs? What might you be doing more of, differently, or better? What *could* you be doing, not just what *should* you be doing? And what are the financial tethers that might come with following those possibilities? Starting to think about financial tethers is part of how you'll go from dreaming your big dreams to living the real thing.

CHAPTER THREE

FROM DREAMING TO BUDGETING: A CONCRETE PLAN

I look back fondly on my work with Marissa, a young woman who had recently finished college and wanted to move to New York City when I started to work with her. She reminded me of myself as a young woman. The first step was to find a good job, so we focused on her resume, LinkedIn profile, and networking skills. Her passions were fashion and food, and she was seeking a position that involved one or both. We also talked through three related questions:

- How much will it cost me to live in New York for a year?
- With that in mind, what kind of salary will I need?
- What does that say about the kind of jobs I should be pursuing?

In my work, I meet young people all the time who are enthusiastic about a job and then realize it doesn't cover their financial needs. We wanted to avoid that trap. By working out her cost of living, Marissa narrowed her search to jobs that would pay her what she needed. She ultimately got a job at a tech company that incorporated her love of restaurants and the food scene. And when she took that job, she already knew what she would need to live and was able to ask for it—and get it.

Now, after five years of being frugal, living with two roommates, and saving, she is ready to live on her own. She has substantial savings for a 28-year-old, which sets her up for more significant wealth later. She's comfortable figuring out new areas of professional finance, from her retirement accounts to her company stock-option plan. And she's in a position to ask herself, "What's next? Do I want to think about investing in an apartment? If so, what do I need to buy my first home?"

How did we make that happen? I'll say it again: we worked backward. You can do the same with any goal you've set. Maybe your dream is to contribute to society by working for a nonprofit. Maybe you're 25 years old and want to own your own house by 35, or take a year off to travel by 30, or be work optional by the time you're 50—whatever it is that's going to lead to a rich, juicy life, surrounded by all the people you care about.

You start with your goal, then make a list of follow-up questions to go with it: How much am I making now? What are my current expenses? How much will it cost me to take that time off? What style of travel do I imagine in my exploration of the world?

Spend time plugging in numbers. They don't have to be absolutely accurate; rough estimates and basic research are your friends here. Once you figure out what a down payment for a home generally costs in your ideal neighborhood, or more or less what it costs to backpack across Eastern Europe for six months, then your task becomes a matter of some simple math. Don't be afraid of the math! We'll do it together.

Let's say you're like Marissa: You want to move to New York City, and you want to live in Manhattan, preferably with no more than two roommates.

You aren't sure how much you'll need to make rent, feed yourself, and have enough for daily life. Fortunately, in the age of the internet, everything is knowable, including the amounts you'll need to pay to live your life: rent, food, transportation, healthcare, utilities, savings, student loan debt, etc. Once you have an idea of what you want, it's not hard to figure out what it will cost you. (Even if you are older than Marissa, building a life in a new city, exploring a new relationship, or making a career change, many of these steps should be the same.)

Start with a Google search, and if you know a couple of people in the town you want to move to, reach out to them for further insight on neighborhoods, whether you need a car or whether public transportation will be enough, and what it costs to go out to some of their favorite places. You might ask how people get together. For example, when I lived in New York, my friends and I typically met up at bars, restaurants, and clubs. On weekends, we went to brunch, hung out in Central Park, or went to the beach. When I moved to San Francisco, friends regularly got together for hikes and potluck dinner parties. I spent less money on going out, but I needed a car—so my priorities shifted from allocating money for restaurant meals and beach houses to buying my first car. Here's how your math might work out:

- Rent for a two-bedroom in a large city could average $2,800 a month. Since you're planning to have one roommate, calculate your rent at $1,400.
- The average utility bill (electricity, water, gas) is $300, divided by two equals $150.
- Groceries for one cost about $425 per month.
- Transportation—a public transit card ($132, unlimited, 30 days), plus $50 for occasional Lyft rides—would be $182.
- Work lunches add up. If you can take your lunch, that will help save money; lunch can average $15–20 a day, or $200–400 a month.

IT'S TIME TO TALK

- Don't forget clothing and fun! For this example, I'm assuming an additional $1,000.
- Add additional costs such as a cell phone bill and Netflix. Student loan payments need to be figured in if you have them. (Assume: cell phone, Wi-Fi, and Netflix are $200; student loan $512.)

This adds up to just over $3,800 in expenses a month. If we multiply by 12 months, that brings us to $45,600. But then there're taxes and savings to think about. Between 5% and 20% of your gross pay should be allocated there. And some states have higher tax rates than others. I picked Indiana for this example; young, ambitious women live everywhere! If your tax rate is 20%, and you save $7,500 in your 401(k) or IRA each year (which brings down your taxable income), that means you'll need to have a gross salary of at least $73,000. So that should be your absolute bottom number.

> I've mentioned "net" earnings a couple times now. What is *gross* versus *net*? "Gross" refers to your salary number before any deductions; "net" is what lands in your bank account after payroll tax deductions such as federal, state, city, Social Security, and Medicare taxes. Additional deductions for health insurance and your 401(k) contribution will also come out of your paycheck before you receive it. When you apply for a loan, banks want your gross salary. When you get a job, the salary they offer you is a gross number, and when you calculate your savings, you should base it on your gross salary.
>
> Net salary is what lands in your bank account after all those deductions. Most people are surprised by how much is taken out when they begin to get their first paychecks, so be sure to adjust your savings goals and math accordingly. The Federal and State Income Tax Salary Calculator is a useful tool to help you calculate your net pay.

Grab the Dream Paper from the last chapter for reference and start a new version. This time we'll put some numbers next to those dreams. In one column, write down all your expenses, so you start to have a picture of what's happening with your money every month. Start with where you're living now. Whether it's with your parents or in your own place, you know what your life costs. Add up utility bills, rent, grocery bills, insurance, school loans, and savings.

Then, in another column, do some research. Let's say you want to be work optional by the time you're 50, and you're 25 now. What is the inflation rate you should be expecting? Where would you want to retire, and what is the cost of living there? How much would it cost you to travel around the world, in train tickets, hotels, hostels? What food will you eat? What kind of insurance would you need? From there, do the rest of the math. How much extra money do you have every month to set aside toward that goal? If X is how much you make every year, and Y is all your expenses, then Z is how much you can save. X − Y = Z, or in other words, Income − Expenses = Savings.

Be realistic about this last part. Maybe you're making so little that you believe there's no way you can pay the rent, feed yourself, pay utilities, and save money. If that is just where you are right now, figure out an amount you *can* save. Can you do this in three years, or is it going to take you five? Seven? Ten? No matter your current level, the important thing is to start connecting the dots by getting it on paper.

WHAT ABOUT A MORE GENERAL BUDGET OR SPENDING PLAN?

I know "budget" can feel like a bad word for many people, conjuring images of endless spreadsheets and late nights hunched over old-fashioned adding machines. It's okay if the idea feels stressful to you or if you don't know how to start. Why bother trying something that might feel restrictive or scary? Because creating your roadmap, dreaming, prioritizing, and identifying values is laying important groundwork—and on the other side of it are all those dreams we just explored.

I'll let you in on a secret: you don't have to call it a budget, you can call it a "spending plan." And the math I took you through earlier is a form of budgeting. Adopting policies and priorities around how you spend your money is another. You don't have to be chained to a spreadsheet unless you want to be, and you can still use budgeting tools to your benefit. Since rules of thumb often feel easier to implement than elaborate, specific systems, let's start with those.

1. Increase automation.

    Begin by breaking a big goal into smaller steps that will build momentum, encouraging you not to linger on the enormity of the task before you. An easy first step is to set an amount to save and then automate. Automating will help support you in this journey by taking the work off your to-do list. Talk to your bank and set up your paycheck so that every month a certain amount from your paycheck goes directly to your savings account. My prediction is that if you don't see it, you won't miss it—and when you do check on your savings balance after a few months, you'll be surprised and happy about how much you have saved.

2. Stay current.

    It's not uncommon for people to create budgets, think they're following them, and then be taken by surprise by their bills, especially if they're not logging into their accounts every month to pay bills manually. For people who struggle with this issue, creating a *cash flow statement* to track spending can be helpful. A cash flow statement is exactly what it sounds like: all the inflows and outflows of your cash at a given time.

But most people I know do not need to keep these statements, as long as they're checking in with their money often enough. When I was younger, I always had an up-to-date checkbook, which showed my own balance every time I wrote a check. Nowadays, I know in my head pretty much what I have because it's held in a small handful of institutions (a couple of banks and the custodian my financial advisor uses). If you keep accounts with more than one firm or bank, pick one of them and import all your information to its platform so you can check on it in one constantly updated place. (It's easy to set up, but if you have any trouble, call their help desk.) A financial advisor should be able to import all your information onto a preferred platform as well. Checking in at least once or twice a month ensures you're in touch with what you're actually spending versus the expenses you planned for.

These days, you can you find apps to help you with this as well. My Generation-Z and millennial colleagues love RocketMoney, for example: on the front page, the system shows your checking account balance, your credit card balances, your net cash, and how much you have in savings all in one spot—plus how your spending compares to past months. But whatever tool works to make sure you're staying current on the what-where-how-much of your money is the right one for you.

3. Start with easy cuts.

If you are looking for ways to save or cut back in spending, start with the easy cuts. Go through your credit card bill and think about what expenses you might be able to *easily* eliminate. What are you spending money on out of habit? What's no longer important to you? Trade driving and paying for parking and gas for a bicycle commute. Forget Uber; pick a podcast to listen to and take the bus, the metro, or walk. Would changing where you buy groceries help save money? Don't start with cutting the hard stuff; practice on the easier stuff. Think of it as a skill or muscle you're building up.

4. **Remember housing.**
   One of the budgeting golden rules is that you shouldn't spend more than 25% or 30% of your take-home pay on housing. Spending more than that essentially shortchanges your future self by slowing your savings and, ultimately, your investments. It can be a tough one to follow because housing is so expensive in many cities with the best jobs. But housing is also a key part of a budget because it's a fixed cost. If you keep your housing expenses to 30% maximum, you'll be more likely to have enough money left over to save and invest. If you need to pay more for housing, search for other ways to economize. Get a cheaper apartment, take on a roommate (or two or three), cut Netflix and cut streaming services—whatever you can to keep your rent low.
5. **Harness the power of policies.**
   In a world that encourages you to spend, spend, spend, saving can feel like a feat of determination. But you can create a framework that will support your self-discipline and help you get to the finish line. One particularly useful tool I recommend is a set of personal financial policies that outline what you will or will not spend money on and in what circumstances. Being clear about your values, goals, and action items is a necessary precursor to effective decision-making in the moment.

   If we move briefly out of the financial realm, you'll see what I mean. My policy is never to eat anything sweet before noon. There are a lot of reasons why I don't do this, some having to do with health, some with how the sugar makes me feel, and some with habits I want to encourage in myself. If I'm at a meeting where someone is passing around donuts and I say, "I never eat sweets before noon," the response is never, "that's weird" or "that's wrong." Someone may think those things, but people rarely challenge a policy. Whereas if I were to say, "Oh, I really shouldn't," then that leaves space for questions and challenges. And if, say, that donut looks *really* good, it also leaves me open to temptation myself.

Setting policies might sound daunting—what if there's an exception?—but they won't be if you develop them organically from your values. If you're someone who doesn't care about what car you drive, you might set the policy, "When possible, I'll choose to buy a used car." If you're someone who is more a fashionista than a foodie, you might make a policy that you'll do your food shopping at Costco, so you can allocate more money to your clothing budget. If you're someone who wants to prioritize buying organic, make that your policy.

Take a few minutes to brainstorm some possible policies that feel right for you. Write them on your Dreams Paper. Then you can work them into your budget, planning to save enough to buy a used car every 10–15 years, to buy a new outfit every spring or fall, or to buy organic vegetables at the grocery store. Again, it's not about anyone else's opinion. It's about what's important to you—and what's not.

6. Make choices rather than sacrifices.

In a similar vein, budgeting shouldn't be about giving up things that are important to you. It should be about eliminating or decreasing your use of things that are less important, in order to be able to prioritize things that *are* important. To all the people who say, "If you're having trouble saving money, eliminate your daily coffee at Starbucks," I say: "If Starbucks gives you joy, buy your coffee at Starbucks, just budget for it. Then enjoy the hell out of that Frappuccino!"

You might choose to bring your breakfast and lunch to work every day so you can go out to a nice dinner twice a month. You might opt not to buy an extra pair of shoes and instead donate the cost of those shoes to a charity you really believe in. You might decide to shop at thrift stores because you think it's greener and because it will help you save money that you can spend on travel. Creating these habits and sticking to them will help you follow the values that are important to you, even as your obligations and choices multiply.

It's definitely a shift in mindset. Instead of feeling like you have to shop at thrift stores because you can't afford someplace else, you *choose* to because it's aligned with your values and allows you to put money aside for something else. Think how powerful that feels! It's not a sacrifice to bring lunch every day if it can help you or somebody you care about. It *feels* good. You've *chosen*. You feel almost virtuous.

7. Spend with joy.

All these rules of thumb lead to joy. I'll say it again and again: I won't judge how you spend your money. If Starbucks brings you joy, or designer clothes bring you joy, or fancy cars bring you joy, then great! The key is to create a financial life for yourself in which that joy fits into what you can afford. Finding joy and living within your means is not an either/or choice. It's a both/and.

In fact, it's essential to budget in a cushion for fun. If you're saving, having a fun fund (5–15% of your take home, say) is crucial. It's much easier to save if you have a specific allotment of money that you are spending on yourself to do whatever you want. No one wants to live in deprivation forever. And if you know everything else is taken care of, then you can feel totally free to spend your Fun Fund freely.

8. Bonus tip: visuals help.

Saving doesn't have to be difficult. Short circuit your temptations with meaningful visuals. To help things along, create a vision board with an image to go with each goal you make—the view from that Tahitian resort, the model of that car you want to buy, a key that might go to your future house. Tape it on your refrigerator or somewhere else you'll see it. That reminder will help you keep on track.

HOW TO SAVE FOR MULTIPLE THINGS SIMULTANEOUSLY

One of the elements that make our financial lives complex is that we're rarely saving for just one thing at a time. At minimum, you'll want to build up your emergency fund at the same time you're socking money away in an IRA or company 401(k) plan, and chances are you'll have other goals over the years that exist simultaneously.

I know that considering how to approach them can feel overwhelming, in part because many people think of savings as one pot. I make money, I put it away in an account, and that means I'm saving! But how about thinking about it as multiple pots? I'm saving for a car. I'm saving for my retirement. I'm saving for my emergency fund. I'm saving for this trip. I'm saving for a house.

Don't just think about it that way; set up your bank account to reflect that frame of mind. You can ask your bank to open new subaccounts, or even just open a new account across town. Then, as I suggested earlier, automate your paychecks to make sure a certain amount goes into each of those pots. Remember to let automation serve each of your goals so you don't have to think about it. It is easier to have the money automatically go into your various savings goals, then manually transferring the money every month.

It's also important to remember that these goals, especially the shorter term ones, are temporary. In the case of an emergency fund, you figure out how much you need to support yourself for six months and then set that goal. Once you get there, you're done, and you get to check that box. Anything over your goal for one pot can go to fill a different pot. Choose a few pots at a time, a good mix of longer and shorter term goals. When you've reached them, choose a few more or add to one of the pots that you want to increase.

BUDGETING FOR FREELANCERS

In this age of gig work, there are more freelancers out there than ever. I've heard an awful lot of freelancers and gig workers say they have no idea what they're going to make in a given year, but I'd challenge that. If you're doing the work for more than a few years, you'll start to see trends if you look for them. Where did your money tend to come from in the last few years? What gigs were repeatable, and what was a one off? If you take the time to look, you'll start to get an idea of what your income tends to be—and how that compares with what it is you need. Don't let the unpredictability of the larger market stop you from seeing the patterns that are already there.

Note especially that if you're trying to figure out budgeting with some earning flexibility built in, you might catch yourself saying, "Well, I need [X] amount for rent, utilities, food." And if you're consistently earning that much, you might think, "Phew, I did it" and leave it there. Don't fall into the trap of just budgeting the bare minimum, or you'll never get ahead.

Instead, back up a little to see what amount you actually need for living *and* saving. Of course, you can live beyond your means in any kind of job, but as a gig worker, it might be harder to tell you're doing that, since you don't always know where your money's coming from. That means you need to do the extra work to understand where your sources of money are and how reliable they are.

Doing that work might also help you realize you're not charging enough for your services. In that case, it might be time to increase your rates. (See Chapter 8, Your Money and Your Boss, for more on that.) Don't be afraid to write to your clients: "It's that time of year! I'm reevaluating my fees, and starting January 1, my rate will be …"

SAVING FOR FREELANCERS

You might think my "different pots for different goals" technique won't work for you as a freelancer, but think again. Most gig workers have multiple sources of income (i.e., gigs), a set up that actually lends itself very well to this kind of saving.

Your first step will be looking at your big financial picture. What do each of your gigs pay you, monthly or annually? How do they stack up against each other, and when do they tend to pay more—particular days of the week or times of year? Make a list: Gig A pays me X amount, which is 40% of my salary; Gig B pays me Y amount, which is about 10% of what I make. Then consider what you want your financial picture to look like, including your top five financial priorities/goals. They can be smaller, like making sure you have enough money for your fun fund, or big, like buying a house. (Yes, I believe gig workers are perfectly capable of buying houses!)

Finally, start matching up your goals to your income streams. For example, a lot of people use apps to tip these days. If you're a hairdresser, or anyone else getting tips, then you have an easy way to direct that stream of money where you'd like—like into your long-term savings. Maybe you'll designate Venmo for savings, PayPal for your fun fund, Zelle for saving for a house. Or money you get from driving Uber will go toward your dream vacation, but income from your editing business will be earmarked for your emergency fund. It's like having an old-fashioned coffee can of cash. But it's virtual, which makes it even easier to automate so it ends up in the place you want it to go.

BUDGETING WON'T SOLVE EVERYTHING

Budgeting is important, and it's helpful. But I understand that we're not talking about something easy here. You can't budget away financial precarity and the anxiety it creates.

My first few years out of college I ate a lot of peanut butter sandwiches and chicken soup because it was cheap. To get around, I took the bus, walked, or took the subway; taxis were a luxury that were mostly out of my price range if I wanted to eat.

Later, when my money was going to my kids' tutors and piano lessons and new shoes for quickly growing feet, I remember standing in a store and thinking, "Where did all my spending money go? I used to be able to shop here." I was always pretty good at quickly altering my spending patterns when I was making less, and saving more when I had more, but sometimes things change so fast that it's hard to keep up.

Even today, when I have a lot more financial padding, that anxiety lingers. If I'm buying something, I worry about it fitting into my budget. I still feel worried about retirement and regularly check my account balances, questioning myself, running the kinds of models I'd usually run for others.

I share this with you because I want you to understand that some degree of financial anxiety is normal. Our goal for budgeting is not to make all your worries disappear entirely. Even if you're in a better place now but you've been through difficult financial times in your life, your financial anxiety may never dissolve completely. And if you're struggling to make ends meet now, no amount of budget techniques can take that stress away—*but don't underestimate how much it can help.* Getting it down on paper so you can see your situation spelled out can help you feel less overwhelmed.

As we'll discuss in the next chapter, part of managing our money and our difficulties talking about it is making peace with parts of ourselves that want to protect us from risk and pain. The important thing is not to let it take over entirely. You deserve a life where your money worries are a little bit quieter than they once were.

CHAPTER FOUR

TAKING A RISK: INVESTMENT AND DEBT

Maxine, a woman in her fifties, got divorced a few years ago and decided to move to Southern California. She had received a significant financial settlement, and the first thing she wanted to do was buy a house and pay for it in cash because she didn't want to have a mortgage. It's not uncommon for people in similar situations to get this idea. They think, "I've got this money; I can buy a house, pay in cash, and I'll be safe." I understand that, but I push back when I hear people thinking that way. If you put too much of your money into a house, you take away a lot of what we in the industry call "liquidity." That's money you can't easily access in an emergency—and money that can't be invested and growing elsewhere.

Maxine was in Los Angeles, where the average home price is $1 million. (Of course, housing costs vary wildly in the United States;

near Buffalo that number can be as low as $200,000. But this example is still illustrative, even if the numbers where you live are different.) Maxine had received $2 million in her settlement and was considering putting fully half of it into a house. If instead she put down 20% and got a mortgage, she would have the rest to invest in a stock and bond portfolio. With a sustainable distribution of 4%, she could receive $72,000 a year—much more than the $40,000 she would receive if she had paid for the house in cash. The difference could have a big impact on her quality of life.

We are a society that is often fearful of debt. It's a fear that makes sense in many ways: debt can be ruinous in the wrong circumstances. But in not making use of what we might think of as "good debt," Maxine may diminish her chances of building wealth. Her house may go up in value; and she might benefit from some tax deductions from having a mortgage. The choice to pay cash in order to avoid debt could negatively impact her finances in the long run.

In this chapter, we'll talk about debt, investment, and the fear we often feel when we take risks with our money. Learning to navigate this emotion helps you make more responsible choices about your money and better prepares you for the similar fear and anxiety that money conversations can evoke.

A BALANCED APPROACH

If you're maxing out your retirement accounts, you've taken care of your emergency fund savings, and you're starting to have extra take-home pay to invest, you're ready to build wealth beyond the basics. What's your next dream? Are you going to travel? Do you want to go to cooking school? Would you like to buy an investment property, a house for your mother, or a home for yourself? All of that can be achieved through savvy investments.

For a lot of people "investment" is as intimidating a word as "budgeting." But remember that if you are putting money into your company 401(k) or in your personal IRA, you're actually *already* investing. If you still feel hesitancy around this topic, consider what you're afraid of. You may think, "I want my money in the bank, in a savings account, where I can see it. It will be safe there." But having your money in a savings account, which usually pays very low interest rates, can be risky too. Inflation eats away at the buying power of money. Consider that $1,000 today will have less buying power a years from now.

Stock and bond markets do not and should not go up in a straight line. Corrections can be painful. But over time, investing in a diverse number of investments will typically result in better returns than leaving your money in a savings account.

So, ditch the equivalent of a piggy bank, in favor of an investment approach that is *risk informed*. Different investments have different return expectations, so having a diverse portfolio, and understanding how the different investments are expected to perform, can help you create a plan to meet your goals. As you review each goal, first ask yourself when you'll need this money. If you'll need it in 40 years, and you're not planning to touch it until you retire, consider investing that money in a balanced growth portfolio that is likely to grow in the years ahead. But if your time frame is shorter—you're saving for a down payment on a house, for example—you don't want all that money in the stock market. Stocks historically outperform bonds and cash, but they also can change value quickly. If there's a big market correction and your portfolio declines significantly in value, that could really throw off your plans. Thus, money you need in two to five years should be invested fairly conservatively.

The second aspect to consider is how much risk and volatility you can live with: your "sleep at night" factor. A well-diversified portfolio is often less volatile. "Diversified" means investing in stocks, bonds, and mutual funds across a variety of countries, industries, and company sizes. To calculate your balance of stocks and bonds, a popular formula is "100—[your age]." (For example, if you're 25 years old, an ideal balance is roughly 75% of your account in stocks and the remaining 25% in bonds.) When you're young and not planning to tap this money for many years (i.e., until retirement), if your stock investments go down, they will have more time to recover. Then, as you get older and you're closer to retirement, greater stability makes more sense so you know your funds will be there for you when you need them.

In general, I recommend starting by investing in exchange-traded funds, better known as ETFs. (These are "baskets" of investments, similar to mutual funds, that trade like stocks.) If you want to invest in a specific stock, make sure to do a lot of careful homework so you understand what you are buying and what the risks might be.

When I was younger, I got excited about one particular stock. I thought I understood it well, and I bought a lot of it … , but then the company went bankrupt when a competitor pushed it out of their market, and my investment went to zero. I realized that effectively investing in individual stocks would require much more time researching each company and its market—and that I didn't have the time or inclination to do that for every stock in my portfolio. That is when I began to invest in a diversified set of mutual funds and ETFs instead.

Today, if I want to try a riskier investment, my guideline for myself is that for every $10 I invest, I put aside $1 for something that's riskier and might have an outsize return. This approach limits the bigger risks to 10% or less, so that if the investment does not do well, that loss doesn't devastate me or my portfolio.

In my personal finance workshops, I often share four examples of how different people might save and invest over the same period, and I compare their results, which are illuminating.

- *Consistent Karen* invests $200,000 from ages 25 to 65, earning 6%. Her ending portfolio is $820,238. Over 40 years, her investment quadrupled because she took on some risk and kept at it over time.
- *Conservative Cathy* saves $200,000 from ages 25 to 65 in cash, earning 2% interest. Ending portfolio is $308,050. She was a good saver, but she kept her money in savings accounts with low interest rates instead of investing, and her bank account suffered.
- *Quick Start Kyle* invests $50,000 (a quarter of Cathy's amount!) from ages 25 to 35 and earning 6%, but he's not able to continue adding to his pot after that. Still, by the time he's 65, his 10 years' of savings is worth $401,008, significantly more than Cathy.
- *Better Late Than Never Noah* invests $150,000 from ages 35 to 65, earning 6%. Lots of people are like Noah and start late. He still ends up with $419,008 because he kept at it once he started.

A few other tips:

1. Your **emergency fund** should stay in a money market fund or a high-yield account at the bank or credit union, since you'll need to be able to access the money quickly in case of an emergency. If you have a bigger fund, say 6–12 months of emergency savings, you might put some of those funds in a short-term CD ("Certificate of Deposit.") Note that while a CD typically pays higher rates than a money market fund or high-yield account, when you invest in a CD, you are agreeing to keep your savings in the account for a specific period. If you need the money before the period is over, you will pay a penalty, giving up some of the interest earned.

2. **"Robo-advisors"** offer another great entry point and an inexpensive tool for new investors. They are automated, algorithm-driven services that can help you start thinking more in depth about your money and building wealth. The program will ask you questions about how you feel about risk and what kind of investments you want to make, then it will create an investment portfolio based on your answers. Many firms, such as Vanguard, Schwab, and Fidelity, offer good platforms for getting started with this. But if you're naturally risk averse, be aware that you'll need to push yourself to take on some risk to achieve growth. A robot can't be kind but firm in advising you about risk the way a human would. (We'll talk more about robo-advisors in Chapter 7.)
3. Once your investment account balance grows to $100,000 or above, and your financial life gets more complex, consider hiring a **financial/investment advisor**. We'll delve into this topic in Chapter 7. For now, I'll say that if you are at this point, your investment institution (i.e., your bank or brokerage firm) may offer you an advisor, but vet these advisors as carefully as you would any candidate. Just because someone is convenient and available doesn't mean she's right for you! Some brokers will want to sell you products that may not be the best fit, such as risky stocks or funds with high fees.
4. As mentioned, **ETFs** are a great way to start out. They trade like regular stocks, have low trading costs, and let you participate in a group of stocks that are interesting to you.
5. Consider using a **target fund,** also sometimes known as a lifestyle fund, for both your retirement and nonretirement investment savings. A target fund uses a shifting mix of mutual fund and stocks that is tailored to perform in such a way that when you need the money, it is likely to be there. (They are similar to mutual funds, but while mutual funds also have goals, they don't change as individual investor needs change.)

These funds are most often used as part of retirement planning. You might put money in when you're 30, when it would be mostly stocks, which are higher risk but offer higher returns. Over the years, the fund would slowly shift to a more conservative portfolio, so that by the time you're retiring it would be mostly bonds and other stable investments. But you can also use this type of fund for nonretirement purposes, such as saving for a house or a car. A target fund is ideal for people who don't have the experience or time to manage a portfolio of individual stocks and bonds. The same firms I mentioned with good robo-advisors are also good places to look for target fund options. As always, make sure you ask about fees before you sign up.

AVOIDING LIFESTYLE CREEP

Getting into a more comfortable financial position, where you know you're working toward retirement and your emergencies are covered, is a huge accomplishment. But there are still risks to be aware of. Typically, you gradually make more money over the course of your professional life. As that happens, your expenses may go up too. You move into a nicer home, upgrade your car, spend more on clothes, and buy more expensive stuff at the grocery store. That's *lifestyle creep*: the idea that since you're making more money, you can spend more money. The nicer car, more spacious home, or expensive vacation are great. (How many different ways can I find to say that finding joy with your money is a good thing?) But often when people make more, they feel comfortable spending more and forget that they also need to increase their savings.

Saving 20% of your take-home pay is a good goal for the various reasons we've already discussed. If you make $150,000, and you're maxing out on both your 401(k) and your IRA, you're hitting your savings goals just with retirement savings. But as you make more, simply maxing out on your 401(k) and IRA could be below that goal. So, if you're not increasing your other savings, but you are increasing your spending, you may find yourself slipping into lifestyle creep.

Along with what I've shared about my personal experience with financial anxiety, I've also struggled with lifestyle creep. Both can happen at the same time! If I'm having a particularly good year and I'm feeling flush, I might be a little less careful with my spending. For me, that means buying shoes and clothing or treating myself to books I might usually wait to get at the library. I'll get into a mindset of, "This is great! I can afford this!"

And then something might change. The next year, I might not make as much, and I've got to scale back so I can maintain my savings and investment goals. With this risk in mind, I've made it a habit to go through my spending once a year and reflect on each expense: the Hulu subscription I never ended up using, the daily salads from the cafe around the corner that I could make at home. I make sure to ask myself, "Do I need this? Do I even really want it? Are my circumstances different this year, or have my priorities changed?" For the most part, these items are extras that became dailies, and cutting back on them isn't a big deal.

Your money goals and priorities can and will change. Managing your financial life is an active process that needs to be revisited regularly. If you're a person who is always on top of what you're spending, a check-in once every 6–12 months is probably fine. But if you tend to be less focused on your money, then setting spending and savings goals every month could be helpful.

The takeaway here is that, as your salary goes up, you'll want to keep your socked-away percentage on track. Once you get to the point where you are maxing out your retirement savings, it's time to think about the next pot to put your money into: new investments? a home? What's the next step toward your dreams?

DEBT AND RISK

Investment, debt, and risk usually hang around together. For example, if you take out a home loan to invest in a house, consider how much your monthly payment will be and how you will pay it back. That "sleep at night" factor becomes relevant. There are many philosophies about debt, and many people who've written about them; most of what I have to add is about managing that fear. If you're planning to take out a home or car loan, or apply for another credit card, I encourage you to consider your stress level and your short- and long-term plans. Here are some questions to ask yourself:

- Why am I taking on the debt, and how will it make me feel?
- How long will it take me to pay it back?
- If I lose my job, what is my backup plan for continuing to repay my loan?
- How much will it cost me, in total, to pay back this loan or bill?

I also encourage you to push back against the idea that taking on any kind of debt is a bad idea. Consider the downsides (the "what if's") *and* the upsides: financial opportunities that debt might make possible. What I wanted to illustrate with the anecdote about Maxine is that debt can be a valuable tool to leverage your money once you reach the investment stage—and by that, I mean to make your money work for you. Let's say you're trying to buy a car, and you've saved up $5,000. You could either use that money to buy the car in cash, or you could take out a low-interest car loan, make a down payment of $1,000, and leave the $4,000 in a mutual fund. If during the time you're paying your loan, that money earns you more than it costs you to pay back the debt, it is probably worth leaving it invested. That's the kind of thinking I was trying to encourage Maxine to engage in and why a consistent debt like a mortgage could make more sense for her than paying for her new home in cash.

In my business, we call this "leveraging your assets": using borrowed money for an investment if you expect the profit you make will be greater than the interest you have to pay on your debt. If you aren't familiar with this idea, it can seem foreign and bizarre, a strategy for rich people. But it's one we can all learn to use. You are probably already familiar with some examples, even if you don't realize it. If you use a credit card to buy a plane ticket or to pay your bills, instead of a debit card or cash, that's a form of leveraging your assets. (And if you pay your credit card bill in full each month and get cash back or points that you can use for something else, that's another way you are leveraging the use of that credit card.)

So, when does debt become bad debt? If you can't keep up with payments and interest is racking up, that is bad debt. And if your monthly payments are making you so stressed out that your quality of life is suffering, that's bad debt. Everyone has a different comfort level for how much debt they carry. What is manageable for you could be unmanageable for your partner or best friend. The important question is: How does it make you feel? Is the stress of making minimum payments affecting your sleep? Is your debt causing you to fight with your partner? If so, that is bad debt, no matter what kind or how much it is.

What About Credit Card Debt?

When I'm working with clients or talking to friends who have a lot of credit card debt, I recommend one of two strategies. They're both good approaches.

I usually recommend they pay the highest interest loans back first. Let's say you have a lot of expensive debt. Your credit rating is low. You have 10 different credit cards maxed out. How do you get on top of the situation? First, look at all your loans and credit card statements to figure out how much interest you're paying: 25% here, 20% here, 14% here. Then make two columns: one is what you owe, and the other is your monthly minimum payment. Not paying that minimum really hurts your credit score, so make sure you cover it every month. Then, put all the money you have left toward the loan with the highest interest. Pay off your most expensive debt as quickly as possible.

An alternative strategy is to focus on paying off your smaller loans first, regardless of the interest rate. For many people, it just feels better to be able to cross each of them off as they pay them and have a shorter list. You can also consolidate your debt into one or two cards. Occasionally, credit card firms will offer temporary low-interest rates on balance transfers for as long as a year. Why do they make these offers? They want you to open a credit card with them, and they are betting that you won't pay off the balance quickly and thus will pay new fees to them. (Often these fees are also very high.) Please read the fine print before accepting an offer that sounds very attractive, and have a plan to pay off the balance before the low promotional rate expires and the high rate kicks in.

A Note on Home Ownership (and Debt)

In this book, my primary focus is to help you manage your money with confidence and to support you in having conversations with the people in your life about that money. I haven't included an in-depth section on real estate, but I do want to touch on one aspect briefly: home ownership. Americans have long used home ownership to create stability and build wealth, in part because the government provides so many incentives through tax law and first-time homebuyer programs. Today, many of the historical barriers and discriminatory practices that prevented certain segments of our population from investing in real estate have been eliminated, allowing more people to use their homes to seed their future prosperity.

Whatever the opportunities and barriers, building wealth through homeownership is easier to do if you understand the fundamental ideas we've discussed so far. Meanwhile, though, here are some tips to help guide you to that goal:

1. An affordable (for you) mortgage is generally "good debt": You'll have a place to live, and you'll build equity if the home goes up in value.
2. Consider places you're sure you want to stay in for at least a few years. Between closing costs and the fact that mortgages are structured such that you pay much more interest in the first few years, a general rule of thumb is that you shouldn't plan to sell before three to five years have passed.
3. The biggest hurdle is saving enough for a down payment and finding a place you want to (and can afford to) buy. The second hurdle is making sure you can pay your mortgage and expenses every month. Make sure you can clear both before you make a move.
4. Take the time to think even further ahead than you think you need to. A two-bedroom apartment is often not significantly more expensive than a one-bedroom and gives you many extra options—for example, if you want to have kids, decide to find a roommate that can help with your mortgage, or want to rent your place out down the road.
5. If a one-bedroom is all you can afford in your favorite neighborhood but you want more space and are flexible, consider looking a few streets over or in neighborhoods nearby that are less expensive. If you like a particular building, would an apartment on a different floor give you more room? Remember the maxim about avoiding the prettiest house on the block and going for the one that could use some fixing up.

6. Try to widen your perspective; keep a broad perspective and open mind on what home ownership can do for you. Here are some questions to ask yourself:
   - What adjustments could I make in my life to give myself not just more square footage but more space, more room to grow?
   - What's the potential for me five years from now if I make this investment in myself?
   - What are the ways this investment could open up possibilities for me and support me in living my values down the road?

If you want to learn more, I encourage you to seek out books that specifically focus on investing in real estate, written by professionals adept in this area. *Rich Dad Poor Dad* by Robert Kiyosaki is one classic and a good place to start. Another is *The ABCs of Real Estate Investing* by Ken McElroy. If you have a friend who works in real estate or have heard about a real estate agent that friends rave about, ask them if they might be willing to have coffee with you and share their expertise. As with so many other topics in this realm, building this knowledge doesn't have to be overly complicated or overwhelming. As long as you're thinking ahead and using all the skills you've built so far, you can learn as you go and still make investing in real estate a part of your financial plan.

HANDLING EXISTING EDUCATIONAL DEBT

There is one more type of debt that, like real estate debt, should be thought of as an investment in the future and our long-term financial well-being. Educational debt, which generally takes the form of student loans, can be used to pay for college tuition, an advanced degree, or vocational training. Taking on student loan debt so we can pursue more education can help many of us fulfill our dreams, access opportunities for ourselves, or pivot professionally in a new direction.

Paying off your student loan is almost a rite of passage for new graduates in the United States. After I graduated from college, I had to live very frugally to make sure I could make my payments. I shared my first apartment with two roommates, lived in a less desirable area of the city, and walked to work in sneakers, so I wouldn't wear down the heels of my good shoes. (I only had two pairs!) I think I managed to pay off my student loans in under 10 years.

But today the student debt situation is truly a crisis. There is a segment of the population (particularly millennials) who were, in effect, sold a bill of goods. They were told that the path to success was to go to college, the best college possible, and not to worry about the cost—even as admission fees skyrocketed. The result: according to the Education Data Initiative, the average student loan debt per borrower in the United States is almost $40,000, which with interest is a staggering amount to repay. Graduates are putting off starting their lives: getting married, having kids, buying a home. If you have what feels like a soul-crushing amount of debt from student loans, it can feel like a heavy cloud above your head, utterly overwhelming. Unfortunately, you're in good company.

If you already went to college, it's too late to change the amount of debt that you have. So, what do you do about it? If you're carrying a lot of student debt—or other kinds of debt, whether car payments or credit card bills—make sure your financial management skills are strong, and that you're a badass budgeter. It's helpful to keep in mind how your student loan helped you get the education that has changed you for the better. Hopefully, it helped you mature and grow intellectually, making you a more capable and better candidate for higher paying jobs. Now that you have the education, you owe it to yourself to get a job that will pay you enough so you can pay off your debt within a reasonable time.

These are the same questions we discussed in Chapter 3 but with the added factor of student debt complicating the equation. You will need to be clear about how much you need to take home to cover your loan obligations, as well as your other living expenses, and build that into your job search and salary negotiations.

This leads me to a point I know is unpopular: it might mean taking a job you don't love. As I mentioned previously in my discussion about nonprofit work, it's important to acknowledge that many jobs, especially at the beginning of your career, involve some compromise. Of course, nobody wants to do a job that is truly awful. But sometimes the main attraction of a job is simply that it helps you reach a place of financial security where you will have more choices. That's okay! I've had a lot of different jobs, and my experience has taught me that work is often much more interesting than you think it will be.

And let's say you get in there and you absolutely hate it—but it pays you enough to handle your debt. I recommend thinking carefully about what it is you hate. Even if it's not your favorite job, is there anything you can learn while you're there? Can you do it for a year, so it can help you get a jump on your loans, then go somewhere else and spend time on things you find more rewarding?

Smart Saving for Education

If you have children or grandchildren and anticipate paying for some or all of their college education, one key tool available to you is a 529 plan, a specialized savings plan for higher education. Anyone can set up a 529 plan on behalf of someone else. The money you put in grows, and you're not taxed on that growth—kind of like a 401(k) but for school. Of course, the earlier you start saving, the better, but the best time to start is now, no matter how late "now" is.

There are limits to what you can and can't do with a 529 and limits to how much you can put in each year, so it's worth talking to your

> financial advisor or learning yourself about the best ways to make it work for your particular situation. But just knowing about and having this tool in your paying-for-higher-education toolbelt is an important first step.

CONSIDERING NEW STUDENT DEBT

When the time comes, any educational debt conversation—with yourself, your parents, your kids, or your spouse—should, first and foremost, seek to answer the question, "What do I want this degree to do for me and my family?" You might also talk through these questions:

- How much can we afford in total, looking at our budget, expenses, and income?
- How will it affect our finances if we pay less or more than that amount?
- What is the maximum amount of loans we feel comfortable taking on?
- What job or career will the degree make possible, and how will that affect my ability to pay back my student loans?

Answering these questions will provide you with important context, shaping what schools you or your kids consider and how you think about viable options.

Although there are powerful and positive reasons to go to college, it's not for everyone. In certain lines of work, a college education may not be necessary. One successful entrepreneur I know found that he was learning so much more in his part-time sales job than he was in his college classes that he opted to go full-time in the job and take advantage of his on-the-job training. Many people find lucrative careers via trade school degrees. Salaries for plumbers, electricians, and HVAC technicians have increased over the last few decades, reaching six figures, and many of them come with a panoply of benefits. This is an option you should not discount.

Still, it's true that the path to economic success—and to professional status and respect—has traditionally been through college. Many of us want to see our kids attend college so that they can later maximize their options. We fear that otherwise many jobs will be closed off to them, even those that supposedly don't require a college degree. But college is a major commitment and one with financial consequences that can last for decades.

If a college degree is definitely the direction you want to go, some paths are significantly more affordable than others. You can work and go to school at night; you can go to community college for an associate's degree rather than a four-year bachelor's. In some states, if you complete two years at a community college, you can transfer into the state university system—which can save you a *lot* of money. Another option is the armed services, which can provide prestigious undergraduate education through military academies, ROTC, or the GI Bill, in exchange for a commitment to serve for a set number of years, depending on the branch of the service.

Which option is the best fit for you? Think creatively. As you start to work out where you or your child might study, discuss long-term goals. Is graduate school on the horizon? Does a potential career path require two years of college or four—or additional years of graduate study?

Take a serious look at the typical salaries of the jobs you are aiming for. If you plan to become a schoolteacher, will your salary support the debt you're taking on to attend a private college, or could you achieve the same outcome by attending a less expensive state university? Well-educated, brilliant, hard-working, and successful people come from all kinds of educational backgrounds and follow all sorts of paths. (Remember, you will rarely be asked, "Where did you start school?" Future colleagues and potential bosses won't care if you studied two years at a community college and then transferred somewhere more "impressive.")

But cost is only one factor to consider. College should be an expansive, exhilarating experience and can be achieved at schools large and small. An affordable state university can be a terrific alternative to an expensive private college. Some of the most respected universities in America are part of state systems. Think of UC Berkeley, UCLA, the University of Virginia, the University of Michigan, the SUNY system, and CalPoly, among many others. Many states have excellent schools with competitive admissions and brilliant faculty. There's no reputational sacrifice in graduating from a good state university, and you'll reap the rewards of being part of a diverse, stimulating community.

Whether you believe a smaller college or large state university is best for you, speak with each school and fill out financial aid forms to determine if you can qualify for grants and scholarships, work study, or other forms of financial aid. Many expensive private schools have large endowments, prioritize bringing the best students to their campus, and provide generous financial incentives to make it affordable for the student and their family.

I've raised big issues, thorny questions, and perhaps some existential dread here, but I encourage you to be honest with yourself and your loved ones in this process, even if it's uncomfortable. Taking on student debt merits deep reflection about values, about finding meaning in work, and about laying the groundwork for a life of well-being, not merely wealth-seeking. And it's likely that there will be additional times in your life when analyzing the costs and benefits of education—and of deeply satisfying work—will deserve your attention and your creative thinking. Better to talk it through now than to wake up over your head in debt without a plan forward.

CHAPTER FIVE

MAKING A MARK: GIVING TO CHARITIES AND POLITICAL CAUSES

I've talked about the beginnings of my New York City life. At age 27, I was living my dream: great job in New York City, great clothes, great friends. Something else happens when those things are true: People you know are involved in fundraising, or your work puts you on a benefactor's radar, and you start getting invited to charity events. There, you meet people who are engaged with making their community better, and they invite you to be a part of it. Living your values through your money can be both motivating and meaningful.

I didn't always know this. My parents regularly volunteered in our community, as did I. But beyond putting a few dollars in the collection basket at church every week, writing checks to support a charity wasn't something I was familiar with. Charitable giving and philanthropy hadn't been part of my financial vocabulary. When some of the organizations I was volunteering with asked me to donate, I started to write some small checks. Then, one year, while meeting with my accountant, he said something simple but powerful: "You know, you could give more." He meant that as a percentage of my income, I wasn't giving much, and there was potentially room in my budget to increase my donations.

Maybe it sounds like a nothing statement, but for me it was an epiphany. It had never occurred to me to think about donations. I started writing bigger checks. Then, as my salary grew, I built donations into my budget. And when you do *that*, something else happens: people in the organizations you're donating to start to reach out to you. "I've noticed you've given," they say. "Would you be interested in getting more involved?"

I was, I did, and I cannot emphasize enough just how much the work has meant to me. Charitable giving and volunteering have changed my life as much, if not more, than anything else I've done. I have derived great joy and made many new friends through volunteering on committees. To name just one example, as the president of the board at my children's school, I helped raise teacher pay, created an Endowment Fund, and set the school on a stronger financial path. It was work that was incredibly gratifying, and it helped me become part of our school community in a much deeper way.

It may be a cliché to say so, but I feel that for every minute and dollar I gave, this work gave me back an emotional reward worth 10 times that amount. When I think of the things I'm most proud of in my life, beyond my children and family, the first thing that comes to mind is community work. Over the decades, I became an active volunteer at many of the organizations where I had started as a donor; the foundation of my personal community are the people I've met through this work. Later on, I also cofounded Electing Women Bay Area, helping support female candidates as they ran for office and won. My political fundraising, organizing, and volunteer work feel truly like the legacies of my life so far.

I'm not sharing all this because I want to gain virtue points or have you think I'm a good person. And I'm not sharing this just because this is a topic close to my heart, even though I'm sure you can tell that it is. I'm sharing this because living your values through your finances is central to the message of this book. Yes, you're here to learn about money management—your financial world, writ small. And you're here to better handle money conversations, the larger, interpersonal financial realm you share with your loved ones. But in this chapter, we're taking an even broader perspective on what it means to wield money in the world we live in together. Don't we all want to leave our corner of the world a little kinder, better, smarter, stronger? What's the point of having money if it's just for security? Why hold onto all of it when you can use some of it to foster change in your community? Men have been doing this for centuries, and today, our money—women's money—matters. The way we use it to shape our world matters.

There are two chief ways to think about how your money can help you shape your corner of the world. The first is charity, whether through volunteering or charitable donation. The second is political giving. Let's talk about both.

THINKING ABOUT CHARITY

If you're still in the early stages of building up your savings, or if money is tight and you need to keep a strict budget, you may feel that "giving to charity" is out of your reach. *Charity* is a word that is used differently in different segments of society, but I encourage you to embrace it in the way that is most meaningful for you.

The simplest way to approach giving at any level is to acknowledge that nearly everybody has *something* they can share with others. If you really are pinched, give your time. If you have a tiny amount that is extra, but is meaningful and feels doable to you, put that number in your budget. Work up from there: I'm going to give $X a month to an organization I care about. Every nonprofit will tell you that each donation, each dollar, is meaningful. As with everything, if it's important to you, set the intention, and give it with joy.

Keep in mind also that many of your charitable gifts may be tax deductible, if the recipient is a nonprofit or 501(c)3. There are nuances and limits to all this, so as always, I encourage you to speak with an expert—in this case an accountant or the charitable organization itself—to understand the full implications for you. For our purposes, the important thing to keep in mind is that you can both live your values and (often) get a tax benefit.

And remember that your gift doesn't have to be in cash to be extraordinarily valuable. Any person who works in development at a nonprofit thinks of charity in terms of "time, talent, treasure." So, if you don't have an extra dollar that you can give to someone else, what else could you offer? You may have *time* to volunteer but no special skills (yet). You may have *talent*, a skill that would really help your charity of choice. And then of course, if you're really busy at work and don't have a lot of time but can write a check, that's *treasure*. Sometimes donations of everything from office supplies to medical supplies can make a difference. They're all gifts. (In-kind donations can even be tax deductible, if they're within IRS guidelines. Again, check with a tax expert for clarity.)

It may seem challenging to work the time-talent-treasure trifecta into a numbers-only budget. Take some time to fully imagine what your charity work could look like. Ask yourself: What am I interested in, what's meaningful to me? Which organizations in what areas of focus could use my help? If you care about climate issues, look into local environmental awareness campaigns. If you care about food insecurity, volunteer at a food bank. And if you're not sure where to start, ask someone in your social group what they are doing. What issues do they care about, and how have they been focusing on them? Then write out your goals. Start this way: I'd like to—

- Contribute ____ % of pre-tax income to charity, annually.
- Commit ____ hours per month to volunteering.
- Give this much in in-kind donations annually: $____ (These can include donating your old car or clothing you no longer wear to a nonprofit. Think Goodwill, NPR, or Dress for Success.)

Including giving to charity in your budget sends yourself an important message: this is who I am and the life I want to live. And as your savings build, consider expanding your goal to giving 10%, the proverbial "tithe" for many religious organizations. I think that's a lovely number to aim for, whether or not you are religious.

THE POWER OF POLITICAL DONATIONS

I was lucky enough to spend much of the summer and fall of 2020, early in the COVID-19 pandemic, in a small town in Western New York that was the site of some of the first sparks of the women's suffrage movement. That part of New York used to be a prosperous region, thanks to manufacturing and production. Opportunity breeds optimism and new ideas. And where you find those elements—money, possibility, economic evolution—you're also likely to find communities of educated women who are in the position to think about what they want, need, and deserve. This was true in upstate NY in the nineteenth century and in places like Silicon Valley in the late twentieth and early twenty-first centuries.

So, it didn't surprise me to learn that right there in my little town, the Fluvanna Political Equality Club fought hard for women's right to vote in the early twentieth century, virtually around the corner from where I was sheltering in place with my family. Clubs like that, and a sister group in nearby Waterloo, hosted activists like Lucretia Mott, Martha Wright, Mary Ann McClintock, and Elizabeth Cady Stanton. Afternoon tea cups in hand, the members planned the first woman's rights convention in Seneca Falls, a two-day historic event that catapulted women's suffrage into the national conversation.

For me, walking in the footsteps of those women was—and is—inspiring. It makes me feel connected to a long line of women who found the courage to speak up for themselves and their sisters, for the causes that they believe in. (It's also infuriating. I can't believe that, so many years later, we're still fighting for pay equality, paid maternity leave, and access to reproductive care.) If you're ardently committed to a particular cause or causes, you should give your time, treasure, or talent supporting them. Then, it's worthwhile strategizing about the next level of contribution. For me, that's where political giving is especially powerful. It allows you to help treat not just the symptoms of a problem but also the underlying causes.

Getting involved with the political world helped me understand that if I care about the cause, I need to support the legislators that fight for that cause. We have the power to change the world through direct action and through the laws that suppress or support our rights—laws that expand budgets for better education, that enforce equal pay for equal work. If we individually don't get involved and vote with our time and treasure as well as our actual votes, then others who do will have a louder voice, and they will make the decisions for us.

You might believe, for example, that we need agricultural reform to ensure everyone has enough food to eat. In pursuit of that goal, you might donate money to charities that work to help people who are food insecure or volunteer at a soup kitchen. And then you might think: who are the politicians who are working to make sure people have enough to eat, who are advocates of agricultural reform, and how can you support them? One type of support can't exist without the other. Without the people advocating for new policy, big change can't happen. And without your support, those people can't advocate the way they need to.

From the president of the United States to your local city council, and everyone in between, politicians all need to raise money to run their campaigns. If you care about your local schools and their policies, chances are your school board has input. If having music, art, a library, healthy school lunches, and gym class matters to you, then understanding who makes those decisions, and how, is important. Somewhere along the line, there's an elected official doing work you care about who needs your money.

That person needs your vote, of course. But sharing a message, a vision, and a strategy takes money. How much a politician can raise has a direct impact on the success of their campaign, and therefore their ability to make change. Your money helps them pay for airtime on TV, radio, social media, and in newspapers. It helps them hire the best campaign staff to create winning strategies, to get out the vote by canvassing neighborhoods and training volunteers.

According to the Center for Responsive Politics, the average cost in 2018 to run for a House seat was just over $2 million, and the average for the Senate was $15.7 million. Seven years later, a Virginia gubernatorial candidate in 2025 told the audience at a fundraiser that she would need to raise $80 million for her campaign. When they aren't working on legislative issues, politicians must raise money by making calls, attending fundraisers, and speaking with both individual and corporate donors. Legislating may be their primary job, but fundraising is certainly a very close second.

That's a painful truth; I don't like it either. But until we find a way to pass campaign finance reforms to curb out-of-control spending, we must help the politicians aligned with our values win. According to the Center for Responsive Politics (CRP), in the 2020 election cycle, the share of women giving money to political campaigns rose to 43.5%. That's compared to 28% in the 1990s. And the balance of women versus men giving to campaigns is on the rise, women representing 42% of donors in 2024, compared to 30% in 2014. It's time for each of us to join in.

How to Get More Involved

You know I believe that small steps lead to bigger changes. If you've read, heard, or experienced something that you believe needs improvement, let's look at the initial steps you can take toward engagement, transformation, and activism.

Is there someone in your life who's always raising money for someone or something? If you're feeling ready to take your lived values from "level one volunteerism" to "level two political organizing," start by asking that person if she has time to talk to you about her work and beliefs. Ask her to share her story and how she got involved. Then really listen. I find that when I'm starting a new project, the more I hear how other people started out, the less I am intimidated.

If the state of the American prison system is something that concerns you and you have another friend who volunteers with a prison education initiative, ask how he got involved and why it matters to him. Has volunteering at the prison given him any insight into police reform, transformative justice, or the school-to-prison pipeline? What is meaningful about the experience? How time consuming is the work? Does he volunteer with friends or his company a few times a month and it's a social opportunity, or does he volunteer for a different reason? (No judgment on the "why," please. The community benefits whether your friend volunteers because it's a social thing or because it's aligned with his values.)

Whether it is a value-driven or social activity, take some time to understand and brainstorm about how you could join in. The two of you might think about the laws that govern prison sentences and the justice system in the United States, then identify politicians who make the related policy that impacts our country and community.

It doesn't have to be prison education; this roadmap can work for any topic. Here are some places to start:

- Tell your friend: "I'm so frustrated/excited/scared of _____ (the lopsided effect of policing in communities of color/the new things happening with transformative justice in our city/the spread of disease in prisons might affect those of us outside). I see you volunteer at the local prison and I'd love to learn more about why it's important to you." Think about how his response fits with your values and your time.
- Before you meet with your friend, take the time to learn more about the mission of the organization he works with. What is the organization's "why"? Who do they serve? What are their biggest challenges? How do they measure success? What are the political tethers to this issue? How do they raise money? Are they taking on new volunteers? How do they train their volunteers so they are effective?
- Ask yourself: what is the best way to have impact? Draw from your conversation with your friend. For some organizations, the most effective volunteers raise money in support of the work the organization is doing. Others need hands-on volunteers who do a huge variety of valuable tasks. Most organizations need a lot of both.

Once you have some idea of what the organization does and how you could be of help, reach out and see if you could meet or speak to someone there. Most nonprofits have someone with a community outreach role. Ask your questions again and hear the answers from an insider's perspective.

You will eventually arrive at a clearer sense of what you would like to do and how you would like to get involved. Is it raising money for the organization, helping campaign for local politicians advocating for the cause, or working on get-out-the-vote initiatives? Set your goals accordingly. Remember, if everything is political, then no action or donation is too small. You have a voice and a say; don't keep it to yourself.

PART II

TALKING MONEY: NAVIGATING FINANCES IN YOUR RELATIONSHIPS

CHAPTER SIX

MONEY CONVERSATIONS 101

A few years ago, when I was out on a hike with my friend Nia, she asked me a question I wasn't expecting. "Are you on track to have enough money in your 401(k) to retire?" If I *was* on track, she was curious to know how I had gotten there. If I wasn't, what choices had I made that had prevented me from reaching that number?

This is a portfolio manager with deep expertise managing money. She is a peer, and someone I've been friends with for more than 25 years. Still, I was surprised. People have always asked me money questions; that's what led me to pursue this career. But a peer asking me about my own money was something new.

We continued to talk for the next two hours as we walked through the woods. What intrigued me about the conversation that followed was that her questions weren't specifically about my "number," the amount I had saved so far. Instead, they were about my strategy. We shared stories about how we saved, invested, and spent our earnings. We compared ideas. We talked about our parents and their money habits and how we each came to work in finance. We were candid, and I came away with new ideas about what I could do differently. And while she already knew that she'd made several smart decisions, she said she had also gained insights into what she could do better—and she felt less alone.

It's interesting to compare this experience to the experiences I had during the 28 years I spent on trading floors. Typically, trading floors are male-dominated spaces where men talk about four things: what to have for their lunch (food), their relationships (sex), their favorite teams (sports)—and their money. As an outside observer, I noticed that if they didn't know the answer to a personal money question, they would ask their buddies or their financial advisors without shame or difficulty. Money talk among men is easy: unabashed, free, fluid. Not understanding something about the difference between a 529(b) or a 401(k) plan is not a slam on their manhood. They are comfortable trying new approaches and asking questions about things they don't know.

In my work as a financial professional, I've seen this dynamic over and over. Male clients tend to be comfortable talking about money. I understand why. Their parents and other adults have talked to them about their money or discussed it in front of them since they were young. Traditional trajectories implied that a male would earn that money and a male would manage it, so they were included in conversations about it.

Not so with women. We rarely receive this exposure or positive reinforcement. As a result, we tend to feel more negative emotions when we have financial discussions: fear, shame, insecurity, even total shutdown. Instead, women tend to be more comfortable talking about their children or relationships. We share stories and seek solutions about our love lives and our families. We hold each other up through tough times. But we rarely open up about our financial lives.

We may be entirely in the dark about how our parents are planning to fund their retirement. We may not know how much we have in our own retirement savings because we've let our spouses manage it. We wonder but never ask our friends how they're planning to pay for their kids' college. We avoid asking direct questions about money because we don't want to "pry" or because we consider it rude, weird, or awkward. This is a true cultural taboo, one that has become a barrier for any woman who wants to take control of her finances and more fully live, as Mary Oliver famously put it, her "one wild and precious life."

It's not hard to trace the origins of this taboo. Historically, in many cultures, when a woman got married, she became the property of her husband. If an unmarried woman had her own money, and was therefore in a position of some power, she might be considered intimidating by a prospective husband, or even disreputable. On the flip side, if a married woman talked about money, it meant that she was not well taken care of. It was considered crass because it implied need. If she was talking about money, there must be a problem.

Thank goodness we've left those days behind—but taboos die hard. We must learn how to have these conversations if we want to be mistresses of our own destinies. When we talk about money with other people, we don't just expand our knowledge; we broaden our sense of what is possible. A woman in a relationship who doesn't control her own money might hear from a peer who does and be able to come back to her partner and say, "I was talking to a friend about finances, and it turns out she and her partner have both a joint account and separate individual accounts. I think that's something I'd like to try."

This book starts with a review of personal finance best practices to lay the foundation, but that is in part to help us strengthen our communication skills. Communication is as important to what we're building here as money management knowledge.

In this chapter we'll start with the basic conversations you're likely to have with family and friends so we can get into more specific situations later.

START WITH YOUR WHY (OR WHY NOT)

Approaching these conversations can feel uncomfortable. It's not easy to undo decades of messages about what's okay to talk about and with whom. Getting clear on why you want to have these conversations will help. Some possible reasons: seeking greater connection and deeper understanding with friends and loved ones, better life planning, finding out if someone you love needs help, or asking for help yourself.

Once you've gotten clear on *why*, consider with *whom* you want to talk about money. Not everyone will welcome such a conversation. Some people may fear that they will come away feeling that they don't have enough money—or that they have too much. Others may worry that they will be judged for their spending habits.

Before you launch a specific conversation, lay out your motivation for broaching the topic. Otherwise, you might get a suspicious, "Why are you asking?" response—and that's valid. People can't read your mind, and you don't get to have money conversations just because you're nosy. Be clear about why you want to have that conversation and what you're trying to achieve, and weave your explanation into your request. Consider why the person you want to talk to would want to have the conversation with you. What will they get out of it?

If you're still feeling nervous or exposed taking this step, consider the rewards: How great would it feel to be confident asking a good friend for insight into how she manages her finances? What if you could have a straightforward conversation with your siblings about the plan once all of you inherit the family house? How would it feel to know your parents have prepared for their retirement? What if you knew you'd be able to afford healthcare in your retirement for yourself and your spouse, and you wouldn't be a burden on your children? How would it feel to know that everything's going to be okay?

YOUR FIRST CONVERSATIONS

Once you've gotten comfortable with yourself, the next step is to approach a trusted friend and find a familiar place in which to chat. You might go for a hike as I did or invite your friend to have coffee. Open up the conversation by emphasizing that you don't want to know actual numbers but are asking about strategy. You wonder how you could do things better. You might find that instead of being put off, your friend is also interested in having this conversation. In that case, here are a few questions you might ask:

- How have you educated yourself about personal finances?
- Do you and your partner have joint accounts, separate accounts, or both?
- How are you and your partner thinking about retirement? Do you have individual IRAs and 401(k) plans? Do you have a coordinated plan for future investing?
- How are you managing your savings for retirement and college? Are you expecting your kids to contribute to their college education, or will others in your family help out?
- What have you and your spouse done to educate yourselves about personal finance?
- Do you manage your finances or do you work with a financial advisor?

It might feel awkward to initiate the conversation, and it's likely to take more than one try to find the right person to engage with. But once you begin sharing stories with trusted friends and family members, you'll wonder why you didn't try it earlier. It will be empowering. It will feel great!

NUMBERS OR NO NUMBERS?

A later afternoon, a different hike, another friend. This time, Alice and I were talking about how much money we planned to leave our kids. In the same way that Nia and I did during our hike, Alice and I were sharing strategies. But this time I also shared a number. It was in the context of saying, "I don't think I need to leave my kids more than $X. I plan to give the rest to charity."

Right after I said it, I realized I had made a mistake. Sometimes, in these conversations, I will choose to share a number, thinking, "I'm being transparent!" But was that really what I was after? The truth, and the danger, is that sharing numbers is the quickest way to transform a money conversation from warm and friendly to awkward and uncomfortable. In this case, there was no point in sharing my number. Unfortunately, society puts a lot of moral value on how much money we have. Sharing numbers in the way I did can be one way of claiming status in social contexts. The unspoken implication in this case was an assertion of my worth, not just financially but personally. If I'm honest, I was maybe being a little prideful. It would have been more tactful—and more tactical—to stick to something general.

Of course, I'm not the only one who has occasionally let pride about money get the better of me. Many people use how much money they have to play off others, usually to make themselves bigger or others feel smaller. For that reason, my rule is to leave specific numbers out of money conversations because it rarely helps further the goal, which is an authentic connection and an exchange of useful information.

There are exceptions, of course. Once, another friend and I discussed the allowances we were giving our kids, who were about the same age. In that case, it was useful for me to hear a specific number. It gave me good context for deciding whether my kids might need more allowance. You might compare specific numbers when it comes to how much you plan to spend on Christmas gifts this year or to talk about scholarships that might be available for your daughter's private school or son's first year in college. And if you're having a conversation with coworkers about what you get paid, sharing numbers can be truly transformative, especially if you realize you're doing similar jobs at different pay scales.

So how do you know when you're in one of those contexts when sharing your numbers would actually be helpful? The answer is the same as my question a few pages back about *any* money conversations. *Why*? Why do you want to share your number, and how do you think it will land with the person you're talking to? Is your aim to make that person feel a certain way about you or to have an authentic exchange? Do you (or do they) need to know the number, and if so, why? What if you simply asked them how they would feel if you shared the number before you did it?

And if you look at the situations I named earlier, in which sharing numbers is a good idea, they all are contexts in which sharing specifics helped us reach that goal of exchanging information or connecting with friends, family, or coworkers as equals. If we perceive each other as equals, that can lead to other productive discussions: Why are you spending money on X? How did your kid get a scholarship to that school? How are you thinking about budgeting in this downturn? When in doubt, go back to my rule of thumb: no numbers, just strategies.

TALKING TO YOUR FAMILY

Now that you've found a friend or two to share strategies with, you can take that growing comfort talking about money and use it to clarify and strengthen, improving other financial relationships in your life—even the ones that tend to be a little more fraught. Yes, I'm talking about your family.

I know this part may sound deeply unappealing. It's possible you've never talked to them about money before, especially if your parents were too uncomfortable about it to make it a regular topic of conversation.

Many of my clients are the first in their families to accumulate substantial assets. They've started their own businesses; become successful entrepreneurs; or pursued professional careers as attorneys, consultants, doctors, or corporate executives. Many have become much more financially successful than other members of their families or social groups. As a result, those clients are the people their communities turn to first when there is a need for financial help—or it falls to them to recognize a need for financial help in others and respond to it. It's wonderful to be in a position to help your community, and share your financial resources, as long as you remain mindful about how you wield your generosity.

Other clients find themselves in tough financial straits but don't know how to admit that to their parents. They suffer in silence and shame because they don't know how to ask for help.

Regardless of your situation, you want your money conversations with your parents, siblings, and extended family to be calm and rational, like any other conversation among adults. One way you can make sure that's the case is by taking into account the money messages you got from them growing up. (More on that in Chapter 9.) If, for example, your mom always folded the aluminum foil and reused it multiple times, it may be because she learned that habit from her parents, who learned to be thrifty during a particularly challenging time like the Great Depression. Understanding her perspective will help you be more tactful and empathetic.

I encourage you to get curious about how you grew up. If you are reading this book, you're the kind of person who wants to better understand these kinds of dynamics, so dig in. If your family talked about money all the time, you might ask why. Maybe your family had a business, and your parents felt that their kids should understand it. Or if, alternatively, your family never discussed finances, it might be because they had few resources to talk about or knew little about money themselves. Whether they were living hand to mouth or were affluent, they may have been raised believing it was gauche to talk about money.

If your family is one that subscribes to the "we don't talk about money" rule, it's possible they will become defensive when you bring it up. I encourage you to approach them gently and with respect, emphasizing your appreciation for everything they've done for you. While they may not have had money conversations at home, they probably taught you how to do many other things that they talked about all the time—and as a result you have great cooking skills or are confident in the outdoors. Acknowledging what they did well can help defuse their defensiveness. Come to the conversation with curiosity—and come prepared.

Almost every family will encounter a point when financial conversation is imperative. An orphaned nephew may need help with a down payment on a house. A brother may develop a debilitating health condition and need daily nursing care. Your widowed aunt may need to move into an assisted living facility. How do you lead, participate, or even begin this conversation in a way that doesn't raise the tension level for everyone? Ideally, you get things rolling before that point.

Start small. The goal at the beginning is to gain information about your family's financial circumstances and wishes. Any new information is valuable, which means any conversation is good conversation. This can be a low-pressure situation. (No, really! Remind yourself of that a few times.) To get started, reach out to your immediate family members and ask them if they will meet with you to talk about family finances. Oh, and *don't* pick an emotionally charged holiday to have this conversation.

We'll talk more about this in Chapter 12, but here are some ways to start the conversation about your parents' finances, to give you an idea of how these exchanges can go:

- Ask about their vision for the next phase of their lives: what they'd like to do, where they'd like to do it, how they're thinking about their legacy, what they want to make sure happens when they're gone? (By the way, "legacy" is not just a rich people word. All of us create legacy in some way. More on that in Chapters 12 and 13 as well.)
- One of their friends may already be relying on long-term care or healthcare, or maybe they dealt with elder care for their own parents. Use that context to ask them about their own long-term care plans. For example, do they want to stay in their home or are they thinking of downsizing at some point? Can they age safely in their current home, or would moving into a retirement community be a better option?
- Who else knows what's happening in their lives from a financial perspective? Who knows where their accounts are, what assets they have set aside for retirement, or whether they have an outstanding mortgage on their house?
- If they've worked with a financial advisor, you might ask if you can join them for a meeting. Many financial advisors encourage their clients to include their adult children in their annual financial review meetings.

TALKING TO SIBLINGS VERSUS PARENTS

It is not unusual for siblings to take very different paths in life; rarely have I met a family where everyone is in sync financially. If you are more financially successful (or perceived to be so) than other members of your family, you may want to offer some financial support for their education, healthcare, or general support. Or you may not be inclined or able to help them financially, but they may come to you with requests, anyway.

Talking with your siblings about money is inherently different than talking with your parents. Sibling dynamics are usually complicated and continue to evolve as you move through life. Just because you grew up in the same home doesn't mean your values are the same. I've seen money issues prompt siblings to stop talking to each other, sometimes forever. Today, one sibling has more disposable income; one has less. A brother might believe it's important for everyone to go, every summer, to the family lake house because it's tradition, it fosters family relationships, and it builds community. Yet his sister never liked the house, couldn't wait to get away from it, and now can't wait to go to Italy on her vacation. If the parents are now in assisted living and the brother can't afford to buy her out, they will have to sell the house. You can see how that could tear apart a family.

Tensions can also arise after parents die. Siblings regularly have to make peace with parents' decisions about distributing their assets. Disagreements may surface about whether another sibling took Dad's car when he stopped driving, and whether both parents agreed to the transfer of the asset. If one sibling becomes executor, she may be perceived as less than fully transparent about the parents' estate. Or perhaps other siblings feel resentful because she receives compensation for managing it.

So, yes, there's often more at stake in money conversations among siblings. I don't say all this to freak you out but rather to encourage you to approach the conversation with as much gentleness, empathy, and compassion as you can—and to get started on these conversations as soon as possible. Come ready to listen and prepared with ideas about what you're willing to compromise on. And throughout the conversation, keep reminding yourself that those ideas and that compassion are your priorities. It's so easy to devolve into childhood behavior when you're around your siblings. ("You have every dollar you've ever made because you're a cheapskate!" "You don't have a dollar because you *spent* every dollar *you* ever made!")

If you have siblings, you know what I'm talking about. Don't give in to it. Focus on what needs to be discussed and assume best intentions from everyone at the table. I have a few guidelines to help you get started:

- Reach out to your sibling(s) and ask them if they will meet with you to talk about family finances. The first discussion might be very informal. If your family hasn't made a habit of regular money discussions, take it slow. Ask for permission and start where they are comfortable. They might not be ready and might need a lot of time to get comfortable talking with you about their finances or long-term plans.
- When you reach out, be specific about what you'd like to discuss and why, i.e., the summer house, moving Mom and Dad into an assisted living facility, the will and trust, the contents of the house and what to do with them.
- When you do meet, create and share an agenda. Ask for input from everyone invited to the meeting; they may have other issues they want to include in the discussion. Try to stick to a couple of topics, to keep things easy to digest. (Too many topics can overwhelm the conversation.) If new stuff comes up in the course of the conversation, agree to table it and meet again.

- Consider inviting a neutral third party to help facilitate the meeting. This could be your parents' financial advisor, the family lawyer, a financial or personal coach or counselor, or a favorite rational uncle or aunt that everyone trusts and respects.
- Try to get everyone in the same room if possible, but try not to do it on a major holiday. If you have to meet during a holiday weekend, consider the day or two after the holiday.
- Schedule the meeting either in the morning after breakfast or after lunch. People are easier to work with if they've eaten first.
- Keep the meeting to a couple hours with breaks, and don't feel pressure to resolve everything quickly. It may take several meetings.
- Don't ask for or commit to giving anyone else any dollar amounts without additional time to consider the financial implications. Give everyone time to think about the conversation and what needs to be done.

IF YOUR FAMILY HAS LESS THAN YOU DO

You pretty much have to talk with your siblings about money at some point. You can avoid it for a long time, but that avoidance is almost inevitably going to create problems down the line.

Extended family is a different situation: the cousins you've never met or haven't seen since you were 12, family friends, the college buddy that's fallen on hard times and is reaching out. These conversations can be challenging, but they can also bring families closer together when they allow communication and compassion.

If you're a person who has done well financially, especially if you're the first in your community to do so, you may attract a lot of this attention.

That's not necessarily a bad thing; many people find it rewarding to give back to the communities that raised them, and they know their community expects them to. But it's worthwhile to examine how you feel about it—what your financial values are when it comes to charity.

How do you talk with cousins or in-laws asking for help? If you have several godchildren and you're in a position where you can help them financially, what's the way that feels best to you? What's your policy on lending money to family friends? These are all issues you could find yourself weighing, and maybe you already have. It's important to be ready, so you can remain clear-eyed and in control of your finances—and so you have a thoughtful and kind way to say no (or yes!) if necessary. I've gleaned a few best practices from my clients' experiences that might help you here:

1. Consider the future.
   Decide in advance what you will pay for. Will it be sessions with a financial planner? Will you fund a godchild's 529 College Fund? Will you provide the down payment on a car or home?
2. Communicate explicitly.
   When you do give to someone, be clear: Is this a loan or a gift? If it's a loan, what are the terms? If it's a loan, write up an agreement and set up a repayment schedule. You might consider automating payments using an online platform to ensure that it goes smoothly. And be honest with yourself: If your friend or loved one is late with payments or cannot pay you back, despite their best intentions, will it negatively impact your relationship? Are you okay with that?
3. Rely on structure.
   Consider a structured gift over something vague. If your brother can't pay his car payment for a couple months and has asked you for help, be clear on how long you can cover the payment. If one of your friends needs help and has a particular talent as an artist,

mechanic, or cook, hire them and pay them accordingly. Put the agreement in writing to avoid misunderstandings.

A structured gift is also useful for situations in which you want to say a partial no to some request rather than a total no. You also might consider making your financial advisor the "bad guy" in that situation. Blame her! "Sorry, my advisor says [X] is the maximum I can give."

4. Default to a direct line.

   If possible, make gifts in the form of payments directly to an institution, rather than giving the money to your friend or loved one. It can simplify things and make it easier for you.

5. Don't be afraid to say no.

   If you've given it some thought and feel uncomfortable about giving to friends and family, that's fine too. A lot of people believe mixing money with personal relationships is too complicated. Again, you can blame your financial advisor: "She says I just don't have the capacity to give."

IF YOU'RE THE ONE WHO HAS LESS

Almost every family has differing levels of income. Most of the time it doesn't matter. If you run into a situation where *you* urgently need funds, family can be a source of support, as long as you approach the situation the right way. Alternatively, maybe your family members are the last people you want to borrow money from—but the difference in your finances can still become an issue on family vacations, when you go out to dinner together, or when they won't stop talking about a lifestyle you can't afford.

Sometimes, the difference in your bank accounts can get in the way of how you spend time together. Maybe some members of your family want to take an expensive family vacation, and you just can't make it fit into your budget. Well, then, have a discussion. You may initially feel some shame or anger; there's nothing like money (and not having it) to evoke those feelings. But if your family wants to go on that expensive vacation and include you, you're going to need to talk about it.

One key point: this talk shouldn't be about how much money you have in your bank account but instead about your budget and problem-solving the specific situation. Remember that people are more likely to respect money policies than something more wishy-washy. Try, "We'd love to join you, but X is our budget, and Y is beyond it." Don't apologize, and don't say, "We can't afford it." If you want, suggest an alternative plan, but that's extra. Set that boundary, and then let your family members react. They may offer to help subsidize some of the costs so you can still participate! If not, try to suggest alternative solutions that could include you.

Note how much stronger this approach is than coming from a place of constraint or scarcity. It's about how you want to spend your money, not about what you have or don't have. Budgeting happens in all economic brackets. How you spend your money is your decision regardless of how much you have.

If you're asking someone in your family for money, do so with care and clarity—and without obligation. Before you go into the conversation, have an explanation ready, be clear on whether you're asking for a gift or a loan, and create a plan for any repayment. In short, here's why I need this money and why I'm asking for this much in particular; here's how long I need to pay it back. This way, the person you're asking has all the information they need to help you. And, regardless of outcome, both parties leave with their integrity intact.

Especially when it comes to conversations between parents and kids, it's helpful to know that the IRS allows individuals to give away a specific amount of assets or property each year tax-free. (This number changes nearly every year so look up the current year guidelines before you give a gift.) For 2025, the annual gift tax exclusion was $19,000. This isn't a solution for every family, but it is a great way to transfer wealth when kids are young adults and help them save for a goal that is important to them, such as a down payment on a house.

If the problem isn't a specific money issue and is more about how people around you are talking about their money, don't be afraid to change the subject or choose not to participate. People can be especially insensitive around their loved ones. They may have the best of intentions and just feel especially excited to talk about their new boat, house, or dress. If you don't want to hear it, it's friendlier and more graceful to say, "I'm so happy about X, but could we maybe talk about something else?"

MONEY DIFFERENCES AMONG FRIENDS

We've all been there. You're out with friends one Friday night, chatting and eating, when someone orders an expensive bottle of wine—then 20 minutes later orders another. Suddenly, half the table is feeling stressed that they will have to pick up the tab on wine that's way out of their price range, while the other blissfully sips their pinot.

Money differences among friends often play out in small moments, rather than big showdowns. Maybe the friend with a lot of money always picks the most expensive restaurant, fomenting frustration, or always picks up the bill, sparking other kinds of discomfort.

Those moments can be tough to navigate. For me, one of the best ways to handle the situation is to speak up right away, using a tone that's kind but direct. Say something like, "Oh, that's a great bottle of wine, but that's not really in our budget right now." You might say you're abstaining and opt not to drink for the night. You might try to get the point across with humor or play it straight—whichever feels more authentic to you. Or when the bill comes, you might keep it simple and say, "Let's share the cost of the dinner, but we're out on the wine."

Before (or after, for next time), you can suggest: "Hey, when we pick the restaurant, I'd love to pick from one of these three …" Or even, "Let's order takeout and eat at my house," which gives you more control over the bill. It's possible your friend might not realize there's a difference in your finances or that you have different priorities—that you're concentrating on saving for a down payment or on your kid's 529 plan. Potluck meals are another time-honored way to share the cost, and the fun, of a dinner with friends. The more affluent folks can bring the high-end wine, if they want. The rest of the group can contribute whatever suits their budget and taste.

If you're on the other side of the dynamic—the friend who has more than her peers—then the best practice is to bring your empathetic self to all your money interactions with them. Be extra thoughtful about how their financial priorities and pressures might be different from yours. If you are suggesting restaurants, it's not hard to send a group text listing possible restaurants in a variety of price ranges so that people can weigh in.

And if you're the person who wants to eat at a particular restaurant, and you are aware that your friends' budget is not the same as yours, you might consider offering to pay for more of it or to pick up the appetizers and drinks. In that case, be clear and up front about your desire to treat.

Travel can work the same way. If you want to go on a fancy vacation that your friends may not be able to swing, you might consider helping make it affordable for them. (Later on in the book, I'll advocate a similar approach to romantic partnerships, using principles of equity to even the proverbial playing field.) If you're the friend with the fabulous beach house, and you want your friends to enjoy the house with you, invite them to stay. If they want to contribute to costs in some way, suggest sharing the cost of the groceries. You might want to foot the bill for a fabulous sail through the Greek Islands and ask them to pay only for their flights. Start the conversation based on what could work for each person. Don't let differences in financial circumstances, or spending priorities, limit the friendship.

Isn't that how we want our friendships—our relationships, our lives—to work, through discussions and with outcomes that feel good for everyone? That's what talking about money can do for you. It's entirely possible, it doesn't have to be scary, and you don't have to do it alone. You have the ability to steer your financial life, and, in doing so, seek greater meaning, greater authenticity, and richer relationships. It begins with these conversations.

CHAPTER SEVEN

YOUR MONEY TEAM

Hakim and Maya had been clients at my firm for about five years when we started talking with them about the possibility of becoming "work optional." Hakim was a family man who wanted to spend more time with his children. He had a great job and was good at what he did, but his priorities were changing. He was interested in creating a new path, going from full-time to part-time to ultimately leaving work completely, in order to be able to be more consistently there for his kids as they grew up.

It wasn't something that happened overnight. It took time and planning to get Hakim to a point where he was ready to make the transition. Then we set up an investing and savings plan and did the financial modeling to show him that this option could work for him and his wife. Eventually, he felt ready to make the leap.

We were able to work well with Hakim and Maya because when they first came to our firm, we had a series of in-depth discussions, a process we call "discovery." During this process, we really get to know our clients and start to understand what's important to them: who they are, where they're coming from, and where they want to go. We ask questions like these:

- What's your relationship to work? How long do you plan to work, and what do you hope to prioritize once you retire?
- Is charity important? How are you using your money to live your values?
- How do you think about education? Do you want to be able to send your kids to private schools, or is public school an equally good option?
- Are you financially responsible for any relatives? What are family dynamics like?

Once we start to understand clients' values and priorities, we work backward to determine what financial decisions they need to make so they can live the life they want. If they want to send the kids to college, we show them what they need to save every year to get there. If they are 47 and want to retire by age 55, we do the math so that they know how much to have saved and where to cut back on expenses.

In this case, Hakim, who was 39 years old, had reflected in discovery about valuing time with his kids. Knowing this was central for him helped us feel confident about floating the idea of his cutting back on work. He later shared that it had never even occurred to him that that might be feasible. Helping create that sense of possibility was just as important as the math. With our help, he came up with a plan to step back from professional life and spend his kids' childhood with them—and to feel financially safe doing it.

This kind of collaborative support illustrates what your relationship with an advisor can be: foundational, authentic, sometimes even transformative. This collaboration can be a decades-long conversation that makes all the others possible.

Most people believe financial advisors are just about math models and investing your money. The predominant narrative is that our job is to tell you that you should have *this* much money by now and put it *here*, that you can move your money around *this way*, and that it behooves you to invest this much using *this technique*. Yes, that's often part of what we do. But a financial advisor can be so much more.

I spent the first half of this book emphasizing the importance of taking control of your finances, but you don't have to do it by yourself. You can find all sorts of resources out there to support you, from courses to algorithm-driven programs, from fee-only professionals who help on a short-term basis to financial advisors who work with you for decades. And even within the advisor workforce, you might enlist many kinds of experts to support you. Your first step will be to figure out which services you need, then to focus on finding the right person for you. Let's go over some of the options.

WHAT'S A FEE-ONLY FINANCIAL PLANNER?

Fee-only financial planners are the most self-explanatory of the professionals in this field. They help clients make a comprehensive financial plan, including budgeting and investing, usually for an hourly or set fee. They don't typically invest for those clients. Some of the things a financial planner might help you do include the following:

- Analyzing your spending habits and/or helping you create a budget and trim expenses.
- Creating short-term and long-term savings strategies.
- Reviewing retirement goals and helping build a savings and investment plan to meet those goals.

- Offering advice on how best to save and pay for college or a home.
- Helping you calculate how much you can afford to give to charitable causes.

A planner is a good fit for you if you're independent and comfortable doing things on your own or if you're getting started with budgeting and investing and you want to have a better grasp of how to manage your money. Once she creates your financial plan, the expectation is that you will implement it: signing up for your company 401(k) plan, rolling over your IRA, allocating your assets, or picking mutual funds (although some planners will create a suggested portfolio that you can follow). Basically, the financial planner creates the roadmap, with your input, and you are responsible for following it.

Maybe you just have a few questions or could use advice on a specific situation. She can help figure out what you need and present a plan that you can implement. Most plans are good for about three to five years; after that your finances are likely to have changed enough that the plan merits a refresh. If you have more questions after that, you can circle back and pay another fee for an updated plan.

WHAT'S A FINANCIAL ADVISOR?

A financial advisor is similar to a financial planner, but usually the relationship is longer term and deals with greater financial complexity. Many people who start working with a financial advisor go on to work with that person for decades, even the rest of their lives.

A good advisor will help you avoid investment mistakes and discuss opportunities. In the case of my firm, many of our clients certainly could do it on their own, it's just not how they want to spend their time—so they find someone they trust who is qualified to do it for them. The advisor is there through the ups and downs, staying on top of changes in regulations and the market, acting as the quarterback for the client's financial life.

Many financial advisors have specific training in addition to the licenses they need to do their work, so it's worth asking someone you're considering working with what additional credentials they have. (For example, along with Certified Financial Planners, there are Certified Financial Analysts, who are trained to analyze companies, and Certified Divorce Financial Advisors, who help people financially navigate a divorce.) Ask, too, if they have a specialty or ideal client. Some advisors focus on complex tax or insurance planning or work principally with young professionals, women, people preparing to retire, or widows.

To find out what services a financial advisor may provide, check out his website, which should clearly spell out which services his firm offers. These typically include tax advice, budget planning, a review of your insurance needs, education planning, charitable giving, legacy planning, comprehensive financial planning, and investment management. Don't assume any service is available unless you see it listed on the site.

WHAT'S A STOCKBROKER? WHAT'S A FIDUCIARY? AND HOW ARE THEY PAID?

The two major subtypes of financial advisors are stockbrokers and fiduciaries. The distinction is an important one: they are differing professionals governed by separate legal entities.

You are probably familiar with the idea of a stockbroker, a person who helps you pick investments and places orders for you. Most investors get not-great returns on their own, so a good stockbroker can offer knowledge of the market and useful experience to help improve those results.

If you want to manage your money more independently, a stockbroker might be a good fit. That's great, as long as you're clear on what you will be paying from the start. Stockbrokers are usually "fee-based" professionals, meaning they charge you a base fee *as well as* commissions they earn from funds where they invest your money. That means the amount you end up paying in a year may be higher than you expect, and your costs will change based on where your stockbroker invests your money. Thus, although stockbroker fees *can* be low, there is a lot of room for variation. Before you sign on, ask about "all-in costs" and if your stockbroker can estimate those annual fees for you.

> Some investors prefer the option of hiring a fee-only financial planner, as described earlier, then take the plan to a stockbroker and ask him to put trades into place. Others prefer to do it themselves.
>
> That last option might sound appealing. But keep in mind that in that case you have signed up for not just making money decisions but handling potentially difficult emotional situations—like staying invested when the stock market goes down or rebalancing when your portfolio is up. Even experienced investors can struggle with emotional attachment when it comes to money. When the market gets tricky and volatile, it can be a challenge to make rational decisions about next steps when it's your own hard-earned savings. Then, it's especially valuable to have access to someone whose job is to help you navigate those difficult moments with less emotion.

The counterpart to a stockbroker is a fiduciary; fiduciary advisors are legally required to prioritize your financial interests ahead of their own or their firms'. (So, for example, a fiduciary won't invest in a fund that charges high embedded fees to pay its portfolio manager if she can accomplish the same objective by investing in a fund with lower fees.)

Fiduciary advisors aim to choose investments that will accomplish the agreed-upon goals as cost effectively as possible. In contrast, a stockbroker is only required to select investments for you that are "suitable." That means the investment must serve your purpose or be an acceptable choice—but it can also cost you extra and earn them a commission, and that's all within bounds.

To illustrate this difference further, let's say that you are allergic to gluten and you are eating out at a restaurant. When it's time to order, you tell the waiter about your allergy and ask what you should get for dinner. Today, most restaurants have at least one specified gluten-free option. A broker waiter might only recommend it because it's *suitable*, even if it costs more than other items on the menu. It's a perfectly good option, and most people like it—plus the higher cost will lead to a better tip for the waiter. On the other hand, a fiduciary waiter might ask you more questions to better understand your allergy. He will be sure to tell you about the first gluten-free dish. But he may also be aware that the chef is willing to make an off-menu dish for you at no extra cost, or that a certain fish dish also happens to be gluten-free. He is obligated to give you all that information and help make the best choice for you.

Fiduciary advisor fees are usually higher than the standard fees for stockbrokers, at least up front. Many fiduciary firms are "fee only," meaning they charge a percentage of the money they manage on your behalf, so the amount you're paying is clear from the beginning. Some investors get sticker shock from the amount that fiduciary firms charge and don't consider what those fees are paying for. Yes, stockbroker fees tend to cost less at baseline. But you may find yourself paying more overall, as additional costs accrue to access more expensive investment options. Each option has pros and cons. That's why it's important to understand the cost structure of both models before deciding whom to work with.

HOW AND WHEN SHOULD YOU FIND AN ADVISOR?

As your financial life becomes more complicated—with savings and investments, real estate, and perhaps a multigenerational family—you may wish for advice from a real person who is able to listen and focus on your particular needs. Because this can be a close and potentially lifelong relationship, if you're ready to take this step, make sure to interview a few financial advisors before you commit to one. And I really do mean "interview." This is where your "money conversation skills" matter. I'm always surprised how little time people spend vetting their financial advisors. Studies show people often spend more time deciding where to go on vacation!

Your friends may be able to help by making an introduction to their trusted advisors. If they don't have advisors but are interested in changing that, consider making it a group project, sharing the research, and pooling your findings. (But keep in mind that those friends might have different needs than you do, which means that what fits them might not fit you.)

You might also reach out to a coworker who seems to be making a similar salary to yours or who is in a similar stage of life. Ask the colleague, "Are you working with a financial advisor? Would you be willing to share their name?" College alumni groups and professional networks are other good sources of referrals.

If you are not comfortable bringing this up with people in your circle, then the internet is your friend. Searching for "best financial advisors" can result in a long and confusing list, but you can sort by zip code, then use some of the terms defined earlier ("fiduciary" versus "stockbroker," "fee only," etc.) to narrow down your list.

Note that advisors typically specify a minimum required amount to open an account with them. The good news is that this is often a guideline rather than something set in stone. From the advisor's perspective, many factors matter when deciding whether to take on a new client. A younger advisor building up her client base might be willing to work with you, even if you don't meet her minimum financial requirements—especially if she[1] believes that you can grow together over the years ahead.

If you're still saving toward an advisor's minimum, you have some interim options. Robo-advisors (the algorithm-driven programs mentioned in the last chapters) offer a starting point, with generalized guidance and a low barrier to entry. The best robo-advisors are easy to sign up for, allow you to plan for various financial goals, and even let you connect to a human if you have questions. Many also have either low or no initial required account minimum, as long as you plan to add to your account on a regular basis.

Many financial and educational institutions offer free webinars, and organizations in nearly every city have volunteer days when advisors and financial planners offer their services to the community for free. That's a good way to meet potential advisors and get a sense of what it's like to work with them. City and community colleges in your area may also offer low-cost seminars and personal finance classes. They are great sources of both financial knowledge and recommendations for local advisors.

WHY INTERVIEW A FINANCIAL ADVISOR?

As you meet potential advisors, approaching these meetings as interviews puts you in the driver's seat. Think of the interview as serving three purposes: The first is to answer specific questions about how she works. The

---

[1] Throughout this book I have alternated pronouns in order to be inclusive. There are many great advisors of both genders—and beyond the gender binary!

second is to hear the questions she has for you. And the third is to see whether you feel a positive connection. All three of these areas will give you important insight into how your advisor will work with you, how available she will be to address concerns when you have them, and whether you two will have productive conversations.

Financial advising (at least the kind that I do) requires intimacy. So, when you're interviewing advisors, the questions they ask you are just as important as the answers they give. Do those questions help you clarify your current situation and your future goals? Has he explained how he will invest your money? Do you feel that he is listening and understanding your needs and values? An authentic personal connection is what enables an advisor to help you build a financial plan that aligns with your values—and that you'll feel excited about executing.

Trust your instincts about whether an advisor is a good fit for you. Before I became an advisor myself, my most negative experience with an advisor involved a gentleman who didn't take the time to get to know *me*. His responses to my requests were often perfunctory, and he never asked me anything about my life or what I envisioned for my future. While women's wealth is growing, it can be difficult to find an advisor who will take us seriously. If you get that vibe, it may be a red flag.

You see, interviewing a financial advisor is about more than the basic practices and qualifications. You're also feeling out whether you can trust this person with some of the most closely held details of your life: if she will treat you with dignity, if your values are aligned, and if she will help you build the life you want to live. Although the questions I'm about to outline are important, the conversation itself will provide the most important data. Listen actively and answer honestly. And go in with a goal in mind. What would a successful meeting look like for you?

YOUR INTERVIEW QUESTIONS

The first set of topics are exploratory, involving issues we've already discussed. Consider them ice breakers:

- How will our relationship work?
- Are you a fiduciary or a stockbroker?
- What are my all-in costs? Based on the amount I want to invest, can you estimate how much I will pay you in fees every year?

Then, you'll want to get a little into the nitty-gritty. Here are some questions to consider:

1. What asset allocation will you use?
    Asset allocation refers to how your portfolio is invested. Essentially, you're trying to ascertain if this advisor will invest your money in a way that aligns with your risk profile and investment goals. If an advisor says, "We're going to invest your whole portfolio in large-cap stocks" (which means large capitalization, or large companies), that could be a red flag—not because that specific type of stocks is a bad investment but because he may not be planning to diversify enough. Another warning sign: an advisor is pushing you to put all your money in an investment that sounds too speculative.

    Really, you want the advisor to talk to you about her allocation and investment philosophy (more on that in a minute) and to use *that* as an opportunity to ask you about your goals and preferences. You're looking for both whether she'll diversify your portfolio enough and whether the response she gives indicates she's going to pay attention to you and your values.

2. What's your investment philosophy? How will you put together my portfolio?

Indeed, in discussing investment philosophy, a good advisor will both explain his firm's usual approach in plain language and will make efforts to understand your particular appetite for risk and volatility so he can translate that into investment strategy. For the first part, you're looking less for a specific right answer—there are a lot of right answers here—and more for the quality of the conversation itself. Does this advisor take the time to help you understand his approach? Does he use words you don't understand? Does he talk down to you? This question is a great opportunity for a gut check.

For the second part, you will want to have done some reflection beforehand about your own approach to risk. A good advisor will not just share her own expertise but will also ask questions about your approach to risk and then offer expert insights to help you adjust your expectations. (For example, some clients who haven't saved enough believe a very aggressive approach will help them catch up. But she might explain that a diversified portfolio that can weather the storms of market volatility may be a better strategy for helping those clients meet their goals with less drama.) Then, she'll talk about how she might translate that strategy into day-to-day management. If she *doesn't* ask, that's good data for you about what kind of advisor she is. In that case, you might want to volunteer this information, and try a follow up: "How will you implement what I've told you about my approach to risk and my financial goals in managing my money?"

It's also increasingly common these days for clients to more actively incorporate their values into their portfolio, to request a portfolio that doesn't invest in oil and gas, or one that doesn't involve guns. Those portfolios are known as "environmental, social, and governance" or "impact" portfolios. If that's something you find appealing, this is a good point in the conversation to ask about it.

3. What investment benchmarks do you use?

An investment benchmark is a standard or measure that finance professionals use to analyze the risk and return of a given portfolio. You might not know the meaning of the term, but you've almost certainly heard of one before: the Dow Jones industrial average, the S&P 500, and the Russell 3000 Index are three common benchmarks. When you're listening to the radio and someone says, "The market was up or down today," they're usually referring to one of these benchmarks, which use representative companies from different parts of the market to gauge broad performance. The Dow Jones industrial average has 30 companies in it; the S&P 500, unsurprisingly, has 500.

Knowing which benchmarks (there are many) your advisor uses may feel a little too "in the weeds" for you, but hear me out. Finance professionals use the performance of these benchmarks to figure out how your investments are doing in comparison. They're making important decisions with that information. For example, a firm might look at how the Russell is doing to see whether it needs to adjust your investments in stocks but would use a different index to assess your bonds. Mostly, what you want is to know that your prospective advisor is looking to standard sources like these, instead of something strange and out there—another gut check to make sure he isn't doing something too unconventional.

This is also a good opportunity to listen for anything that strikes you as too good to be true. She might respond to this question by saying, "Oh, we try to beat the market every year." Sounds great, but how is she doing that? Is she taking on additional risk so that she can hit that goal? Will she charge you fees for having met it?

Or another advisor might say, "We work a lot with private equity or venture capital." Sure, that sounds sexy, but it might not be appropriate at all for you. This is just another opportunity to make sure his responses are aligning with what you want.

4. Who holds your money?
Your financial advisor should work with an independent custodian that holds the firm's assets. For example, look for a firm that works with large custodians, such as Schwab and Fidelity, to ensure their clients' assets are safe and secure.

Ask your prospective advisors about their firm's custodians. Even though somebody else is managing your money, you should be able to log into the website of Schwab, Fidelity, or elsewhere and see that your money is there.

5. What happens if a member of your team retires or leaves the firm?
Since this is a long-term relationship, it's important to understand what kind of transition protocols your prospective advisor has in place. How has she ensured you'll experience continuity across your relationship, one that could span multiple decades?

Ideally, your firm will have a team of people working with you. That means that if something happens to one member of the team, you'll always know somebody else there. And if someone retires, or even if they're on vacation when something urgent comes up, there's somebody else you can reach out to.

Different firms will have different answers to the question of succession. Some advisors work in pairs: a lead advisor and a "support advisor." Then, if your advisor retires or is in on vacation, you still have a close point of contact. You may continue working with that person, or he may recommend another advisor and tell you why. But he'll make sure you're not forgotten and that you don't suddenly get a call from a stranger asking unexpected money questions. Note that a change in advisor is not necessarily a bad outcome. You just want to know what to expect.

6. Do you have training in family governance? Do you provide financial education for kids?

    If you have children, at some point, you may want to bring them into your financial discussions. In that case, you should ask your prospective advisor if she's comfortable with that. You might also consider asking if she's trained in family governance, which can include issues like familial debt or inheritance, talking to your kids about your financial legacy, and more.

    If you're considering whether you want to grow old with this firm, keep in mind as well that financial advisors are sometimes the first people to discern possible cognitive decline and consider asking how he usually approaches it. Some advisors have a form for clients to fill out that specifies a child or other trusted person to make decisions in the case of incapacitation. Your financial advisor should be able to talk with you about this and make you feel at ease about your plans. (We'll cover more about this conversation in particular, and preparation for aging and cognitive decline in general, at the end of the book.)

NEXT STEPS

Once you've identified an advisor who feels like the right person for you, the next step is typically signing an "investment management agreement." That's a nonbinding document that allows your new advisor to give you, well, advice. As part of this initial process, some firms may ask you to pay an initial fee for planning, and then they'll agree to apply that fee to your first year if you decide to stay. Other advisors will do just the first part of the task and then finish the project once you agree to sign on.

The nonbinding aspect gives you an escape route if you find, three months down the road, that this is not someone you want to work with. That's allowed! Then you should be free to sever the relationship. For most firms, it just takes a phone call.

But I hope your relationship with your new advisor will have longevity—that you've found someone you can come to with questions as your life evolves and your needs change. I'm glad to say we've maintained that kind of relationship with Hakim and Maya. Hakim is still working at the same tech company, but he's transitioned to remote work that he can do when his children are at school. He could retire, but he finds the work intellectually engaging, so he's opted to stay part-time, while also showing up for his kids at both pickup and drop off. He and his wife have a plan for themselves and are executing on that plan; when we meet, they tell us they're living their best lives. That's something we made happen together. I'm confident you and your new advisor can do great things together, too.

CHAPTER EIGHT

YOUR MONEY AND YOUR BOSS

A few years ago, I worked with Mariam, a recently divorced client, as she prepared to move to a new city and start a new job. She was going from being a stay-at-home mom to becoming the primary breadwinner for her family, so this was a high-stakes move. After several job interviews, she got an offer from a company she was excited about. But while they were going to provide good benefits, the offer was $5,000 short of what she needed.

Going back to ask for more felt brash and risky; I had to reassure her that it was standard practice. We literally rehearsed the conversation until she felt comfortable saying things like, "I'm excited about this job, but I'd like to have a deeper discussion about the salary offer."

And then we also went through the "what ifs": What if the boss says, "We can't do anything more?" Then, she could ask for other perks or assistance, such as help with moving costs. What if the boss says, "What did you have in mind?" She had to have done the math beforehand and be able to respond, "An additional $5,000 would make a big difference to me, and here's why." She also asked if they would be willing to discuss another raise at the six-month mark if she was doing well.

It worked: the company came back pretty quickly and told her that, while they couldn't raise their offer the full $5,000, they could make $3,000 work. It was a powerful lesson for her. If she hadn't asked, they probably would not have offered—but she did ask. Asking also communicated to Mariam's employer that she was smart, savvy, and someone to take seriously. It isn't a guarantee, but it often gets you somewhere.

This example is an apt beginning in a chapter on money conversations in the workplace. Societal messages about how women should behave play a role in all our conversations about money—and they may manifest especially strongly in a professional context. Mastering our fears of discussing money at work allows us to better show up for both ourselves and the people around us.

IT'S ALWAYS A NEGOTIATION

Let's start with the earliest conversation you might have about money in a given job: the salary negotiation. If, like Mariam, you've applied, interviewed, and have a couple of job offers in hand, then congratulations! It's likely that each of your offers is appealing in some way. One might have the best salary; another, greater flexibility; another, career advantage. Think about what your top three priorities are. If you get two out of three, that's pretty good.

Your next step is to carefully calculate your financial needs, as seen in Chapter 3. Once you've received an offer, you have some bargaining power because you know they want you on their team. Many women have been socialized to resist using that power, while men seem to have fewer qualms about asking for what they need and deserve. Like Mariam, you might feel uncomfortable countering if you're offered a job you want, even if the offer number is under your identified minimum. You might worry that your would-be employer will be put off or even insulted.

In fact, studies show that women who ask for more are sometimes perceived as aggressive. But my response is: "That's fine. We need the money just as much as anyone else does." Most people are not asking because they're going to spend it on some shiny new thing. They're asking because it's the difference between making their budget work or not. If you find yourself resistant to the idea of negotiating, remind yourself why you are asking. Chances are, it's so you can better contribute to your household, support your family, save for a house, or build a rewarding life with your partner. Not that that should matter, by the way: you deserve to be compensated fairly regardless of what it's for.

Many outcomes in salary negotiation come down to attitude and preparation—how we're taught to approach problems, what we're taught we deserve, and how we communicate. When we feel confident in our stance, we can more easily find ways to negotiate positively and with savvy. Let's say you need $55,000, and they are offering $52,000. Approach the person or team making the offer and let them know what you need to make it work for you. You'll be more credible if you show them that you've researched the cost of living in your intended city and have numbers to back up your claim. While this approach won't guarantee you get exactly what you asked for, it will impress them and will often result in a boost to the overall package.

If an overall raise isn't possible, don't despair. It's surprising how many other potential levers can be available to those hiring new employees, especially when the job is not entry level. It's not just a higher salary that can sweeten the pot for someone who has been vetted and selected as the best potential hire. Think creatively, and consider asking your prospective employer to do the same. You might ask an employer to pay for moving costs, additional stock grants, the opportunity to renegotiate your salary in six months, or more vacation days.

That happened to me not so long ago. My firm was acquired, and the new team offered me half of the vacation I had under the previous management. I told them I wanted to stay with the original amount of vacation, and they quickly agreed. I also have a friend who mentioned that parking downtown was going to cost her $3,000 annually and asked if it would be possible for the company to consider providing her with parking. The answer? "We have a policy of encouraging people to take public transportation, but since it's taken us a while to fill this job, we have saved money and can add $3,000 to your salary."

Men do this all the time! As long as you are professional and back up your requests with data, counteroffers can be a useful way to negotiate for additional pay or benefits. Your boss-to-be will be impressed you did the research, know your worth, and understand the salary that can make the job work for you. If you approach the negotiation positively, not defensively, showing that you are capable of creative thinking, she will be impressed with your problem-solving ability. She might not be able to raise her offer, but she might be willing to consider reevaluating your work and discussing a raise in six months. Or she might be able to provide another benefit or perk that helps you financially. Whereas if you take the job and ultimately can't afford to work there, you won't last very long. It won't make financial sense, and you'll be miserable.

THE IMPORTANCE OF MANAGING UP

Fast forward a couple of months. You successfully managed to negotiate your salary up a few thousand dollars and are feeling good. You took the job, you started working, and you love it. Now, instead of getting too comfortable, it's time to set yourself up for maximum success down the road.

The concept of "managing up" will be central to achieving that goal. Although the term may sound calculating, the idea is to establish good communication with your boss early in your relationship. He is probably managing more than one person and might not notice when you do something new, cool, or worth noticing; he may not always have a clear idea of what you do all day. That means it's important to create rapport and an ongoing dialogue so that he is aware of what you're doing.

Your company may already have a review system in place. If so, become familiar with how it works. If it doesn't, ask your boss what works for her. It can be helpful to have a conversation with or send an email to your superior(s) at the end of each week, month, or couple of months, letting them know what you've accomplished. Getting the tone right is important; you don't want to come across as bragging. Take note of any reply and adjust according to the signals you get. But as a starting point, a summary update is always a great way to highlight what you've done. When you can, include praise for others on your team. It builds goodwill all around.

Let's say you're working in sales, and your job is to bring in new clients and develop new markets. You might send an update to your boss once a week or month saying, "I had [X number] of sales calls. I networked with [X number] of providers. These were the outcomes. This is how I moved forward with [X] sales relationship." (Using sales management software tools that keep track of your activity will also support your story. Just make sure to regularly update your reports so they are accurate.)

This kind of update is especially important if you, like so many Americans, work remotely. If your boss isn't seeing you regularly face to face, how is he going to know how many calls it took to bring in that big new account? If you were brought in to leverage your tech skills to launch a new project—maybe a social media presence or some project management software—make sure to let your supervisor know how you are picking up followers, growing your audience, or helping your colleagues prioritize and meet deadlines as a team.

Since most people don't do it, if you're the person who *is* going through the trouble of providing these updates, then your boss is going to have greater awareness of your contribution. That's good news for you, financially and professionally, in the long term.

As you work to build a relationship with more senior and experienced coworkers, don't feel like you need to wait until you have positive news to report. Seek them out for an occasional problem-solving session when there's a challenge you'd like advice on. It may sound bold to invite your boss or more senior colleagues to coffee, but many managers would be receptive to this kind of positive, less formal interaction.

HOW TO ASK FOR A RAISE

So many of us find the prospect of asking for more money terrifying. Why? We're qualified. We deliver results. And we've been managing up, so our bosses are aware of how we are contributing to company growth. What are we afraid of? Let's talk about some creative approaches.

1. Document your accomplishments and contributions.
   In almost every job, when you start, your manager will have goals and expectations for the year ahead. When the time comes for an annual review, draw on those goals and the records you've been keeping from "managing up," and make a spreadsheet of the progress you've made. Gathering all the data will give you helpful perspective on what you've accomplished, and that perspective will help you communicate your story effectively. Hopefully, your boss will also have reflected on your work and will have an idea of what you're going to say, but keep in mind she might not have as accurate

a picture as you're able to provide. That's where the preparation comes in.

If you want a raise, you'll want to start your negotiation from a place of value: here's what I've done for you, for our team, for our organization. You might use internet resources or talk to friends who do similar work in order to understand what the next step is for someone in your role, what other people in your position get paid, and where *you* want to go next. Remember that even though your boss has authority, you get a say in shaping your path as well.

This also means being prepared to take constructive feedback. When your boss indicates there might be room for improvement in an area, thank her for the feedback and ask for specific suggestions. Showing you're not afraid to work toward growth is a positive in itself.

2. Understand the best time to ask.

Of course, a six-month review provides a built-in opportunity to talk to your boss about your position and pay. But there are also better and worse times of the day, week, and year for an ask like this. When is your boss the least stressed and the most likely to be open to new ideas? People tend to be really busy on Mondays, and on Fridays they're usually ready to get out of the office. Don't schedule a meeting just before lunch or dinner. Tuesday, Wednesday, and Thursday in the late morning or early afternoons are all good options!

When you're asking for feedback, try to be aware not only of the calendar but where the organization is in its annual cycle. Think about your company culture: When during the year do things tend to get stressful and hectic? When during the year allows for more down time? Does your organization get busy at the end of the quarter or at the end of the month? Try to pick a time when you're going to have your boss's full attention. If your company is going public in three months and the people evaluating you are heavily involved in preparing for that event, you might consider waiting until the deadline has been met or you have a scheduled review.

3. Research the salary range for your role and your industry.

Many online resources can provide useful insight into the appropriate salary range for your role and location. Sites like Glassdoor and LinkedIn are a good starting place and will give you some baseline numbers. Check industry-specific websites as well.

Reach out to friends, colleagues, and other contacts for more information. I know it can be difficult to approach friends and colleagues on this topic. Even though we've come so far, people are still taught not to talk about their salaries. This is a frustrating and destructive norm that hurts women more than anyone. If you don't want to talk to friends or colleagues, look for networking groups in your field and ask people there. You might also consider getting in touch with a headhunter. They tend to have knowledge about your particular area that's useful.

Alternatively, an effective way to find out about salaries is to ask a coworker, "What do you think the average salary is for this role?" Most people are willing to talk about numbers if they don't have to get personal. They might not be comfortable telling you what *they* make, but they'll tell you what they think the average is. And that tells *you* something in turn, especially if you ask three or four people with similar jobs.

4. Practice your "ask."

Some of you are thinking, "It's too intimidating to ask for a raise; I don't know what to say." But if you've done all this preparation, if you've been managing up, if you've been the best you can be, then you can do this too. I'm a big believer in literally practicing what you're going to say to the person sitting across from you—out loud. Write an outline and then launch into imaginary conversation.

The "out loud" part is important. Sometimes when I do this, I'll end up stumbling over the words because it's not actually how I talk. Practicing out loud will allow you to hear how your thoughts translate to speech and will give you time to course-correct before your big meeting. Consider practicing with a friend too.

Then, go in and listen to what your boss has to say at your review. You shouldn't encounter too many surprises, since you've been in close touch. It's likely to be positive. You might respond with, "I'm happy this is such a solid review, and I'm excited about this work and the firm. Can we talk about how this might translate into greater opportunity and compensation?"

Then pause. Let that question sink in, and let her answer it. Your boss might say, "Sure!" and then you start that conversation. She also might say, "Oh, we don't usually give raises at this point. You've been doing a good job, but I haven't thought about it." Whether or not that's genuinely true, it's best to give her the benefit of the doubt here. You might consider replying, "Well, this positive review is a good outcome. What should my next steps be? When can we schedule a meeting to discuss my compensation?"

5. Don't be discouraged if you don't get the raise today.
That just means you need to create the opportunity to ask again. If your boss continues to be vague or noncommittal or tells you something like, "Just keep doing what you're doing until the end of the year," ask for real metrics or goals so you both have an idea of what *would* merit a raise.

Be prepared to overcome objections; be polite, frank, and assertive. Say, "I'd hate to wait until the end of the year and find out I'm not going in the right direction. Could I speak to you every few weeks to check in about this?" If he says no to that, ask for a timeline over the next quarter to revisit the question. Don't hesitate to create the opportunity to touch base, and consider seeking out other resources as well. Ask your boss if you should be talking with HR as well. Is there somebody else on your team who could help you reach your goals?

TALKING ABOUT MONEY AT THE OFFICE

Sharing money strategies with colleagues can be just as helpful as when you do it with friends or family. But cultural norms push us to avoid the discussion, and company rules can make it extra tricky.

Unfortunately, this taboo means everyone suffers. For example, in companies that pay their bonuses in cash and stock, employees may not understand what that means for them financially. I worked with a client who was a secretary at a tech company, and she had $100,000 in the bank from exercising her stock options. But she didn't know what to do with it, didn't know whom to ask, and knew that HR wasn't able to provide the education she needed to make informed decisions. In that kind of situation, being able to discuss money with your colleagues is essential. At the very least, you might ask them whether they have a financial advisor, or how *they've* educated themselves on investment.

By now, you know my mantra on this topic. You don't need to share your specific *numbers*, but you can benefit from sharing *strategies*. Consider a generic question like, "What are you thinking about when it comes to our stock options?" Or try out, "How did you decide whether to buy into our HSA (health savings account)?" Or in passing: "I see that we've got an employee stock purchase plan. Do you understand how that works?"

In starting these conversations, you might find another colleague or two who also wants to know more. Then, over time, maybe you'll find 3, 5, or 10 colleagues who can band together to ask for more information.

In doing so, you're helping create an environment where it's okay to not know the answer—and it's safe to seek that answer together.

WHAT IF YOU FIND OUT YOUR COWORKER MAKES MORE THAN YOU?

Even with all the progress we've made, it's still true that men in the same roles as women often make more than their female counterparts. And it's one reason many companies make it clear they do not want their employees to compare salaries—even though it's illegal in many states to forbid salary disclosure.

If you suspect the man sitting next to you makes more than you do, I suggest returning to the technique I mentioned earlier. Asking him, "What do you think the guy sitting across the floor makes?" or "What do you think they pay over at [X] company?" can be pretty illuminating, since he'll be answering the question based on his own experience. (Again, resources like Glassdoor allow you to research salary info for positions at specific companies.)

If you find out or suspect that a coworker of any gender makes more money than you, the first step is to find out why. That person may be doing something more in their work that you're not aware of. Your impression might be that you both do the same job, but maybe your boss thinks that he or she brings in more clients or has more experience. Start from a place of curiosity. Why is that person making more, and what do I need to do so I can make more, too?

Then, armed with that information, you can go to your boss. Don't name names. Most jobs do have a salary range, so it's good to acknowledge that. You might phrase it as, "What is the salary range for this role?

What are the metrics I'd need to meet to be paid at the higher end of the range?" Approach the conversation with as much positivity as you can, even though you may feel angry or upset.

Of course, it does happen that two people get paid different amounts for trivial reasons. Let's say you find out that your colleague is being paid more, and it doesn't seem very fair to you. You've gone back and asked what more you can be doing, and you're doing it, but you still feel like it's unequal. You've talked to HR. Maybe you've talked to your boss and gotten some feedback, but you're still not getting paid more.

At that point, I'd recommend starting to shop for a similar job elsewhere. Coming back to the bosses with other opportunities in hand puts you in a much stronger bargaining position.

What if there's no budging, and you feel you are being treated unfairly or even suffering gender discrimination? I'm an activist type. I'm not afraid to stand up and speak truth to power. So, I'm not saying you shouldn't speak out if you want to speak out. What's happening to you in this case is deeply unfair, and this book is, in part, about empowerment.

But I'm also aware that the decision to call out injustice isn't a simple one. Not everyone can afford to plant a flag and make a lot of noise. There are real ramifications to being the person who speaks out, especially for people from marginalized groups. If you're 25, you might be thought of as the young troublemaker. If you're African American, you might be branded the stereotypical angry Black woman. If you're older and used to expressing yourself powerfully, you might be written off as strident. These are hurtful stereotypes, but I know firsthand that these beliefs still sometimes have power in the workplace. I know standing up for yourself can come with real personal and professional costs.

You know what's right for you and what will let you sleep at night. If you feel up to the challenge of speaking up, I'm already proud of you. And if you don't feel prepared to do that, I understand. There are ways to be an activist for yourself besides being the squeaky wheel.

Sometimes, self-advocacy means leaving when you feel you're not being treated well. We live in an at-will economy. If you don't like what they're paying you, you've done everything you can, and they're still not paying you more—go get a better offer somewhere else! Ask for more at your new job and be the kind of employee that they want to hire.

WHAT ABOUT CHANGING JOBS?

The best way to get your next job is by being really good at your current one, while staying aware of possible other opportunities. When a recruiter calls, take the call. It doesn't hurt to maintain that relationship and keep one eye on the job market. What skills are people looking for? Why is the recruiter reaching out to you?

You'll also get a lot out of talking to your friends about work. It makes dealing with interpersonal and professional stuff less lonely, and it provides insight. Ask them questions. What do they like about their jobs? What opportunities are they excited about these days? How are they thinking about their next professional steps?

If you treat every job as a gateway to your next job, then every gig—even one you see as temporary—is a learning opportunity, another stepping stone on your career path. That means never burning a bridge and being the best employee you can be at every job, so good that when you tell them you're leaving, they're sad to see you leave. Aim to operate "above the line" with the best attitude possible every day. You never know who will be able to open doors for you and what might be on the other side.

That's the "how," but what's trickier is often the "when" and "why." This one is tough, especially in an uncertain economy. Still, it's time to leave a job when it's not satisfying for you anymore, when you're not learning, or you're not getting the opportunities that you had hoped for. A job is a relationship, and good relationships create opportunities for growth. If you're not growing, if it's not challenging or interesting or giving you what you need, or if you've been there a while and you don't see new opportunities, consider looking for other options.

HANDLING A BUYOUT OR LAYOFF

It sucks to be laid off. And it can feel almost as bad to take a buyout, even if you've already lined up your next gig. The good news is that you usually get some kind of severance payment when you're laid off, and a buyout also involves some compensation. And neither has to be a disaster if you're prepared financially and emotionally. You have your emergency fund ready, your budget is organized, and you know what you need to cover your costs each month. Add that to your severance from your old employer, and you'll have a cushion to support yourself as you look for your next job. But don't stop talking about money just because you (or the company) are going away! Be just as clear and assertive in your conversations about severance or a buyout as you were about salary and benefits.

You might even ask about a company's severance policy when you *get* a job. When you are talking to HR before signing your contract, don't be shy about saying, "I hope I stay here for the rest of my life, but could you tell me what the severance policy is when people get laid off? What happens if there's an economic contraction? What would I be able to rely on when it comes to health insurance?"

They might be able to share some information right there: "Our policy is to give a month of pay for every year an employee has worked here," or "We give you two weeks' salary no matter how long you've worked here."

That is important information to have in case of an emergency. If you know in advance your severance is only two weeks' pay, for example, you might want to add more to your emergency fund.

Similarly, if you're in a situation where your company is being bought, it's entirely fair to ask about the future of your role: what a post-merger workplace might look like and what your prospects are. Of course, the best-case scenario is if they want to keep you around; then you may have some leverage. Are they going to give you stock in the new company or match the stock you have in your current organization? They might offer you an incentive package or a signing bonus.

Every company needs good employees, and they know you're worth retaining. Don't forget your value! Even if you like your company and you like the people you work with, it's often a good idea to investigate other options. But it might also make sense to stay and see how it feels. You can always leave and go somewhere else after six months if the new company is not what you expected.

THE MATERNITY QUESTION

You absolutely deserve to be able to "have it all," both a family and a fulfilling work life. And that isn't always a simple prospect. From a professional perspective, there's rarely a perfect time to get pregnant. I was named a managing director at my firm within weeks of getting pregnant and wanted to postpone revealing my pregnancy as long as possible. Since I was pregnant with twins, five months was about the limit. I was thrilled; I just didn't want to suffer any consequences due to pregnancy, consequences I'd seen friends and colleagues face. Legally, you don't have to tell your boss that you're having a baby until you're literally in the hospital delivering. But giving him enough of a head's up so that he can prepare for you being out of the office is still a decent thing to do.

Much of navigating this situation well is understanding what kind of boss you have and what timing or approach will work best for your relationship. Ideally, you have the sort of relationship with her where you can say, "Let's discuss a game plan that will work for us while I'm on maternity leave." You may not know yet what you will do once you've delivered your baby, and there is no legal reason you need to disclose it in advance. Still, employer response to pregnancy and maternity leave is so much better now than when I had my kids. Many, even most, professional-level jobs provide maternity leave of some kind. Even paternity leave is becoming more common.

As you enter this stage of your life, think about creating a short- and long-term childcare plan, including possible moves from job to job. If you know you want six months of maternity leave, but your company only offers three—and you need that salary to live—then now is the time to increase savings. Other pertinent questions include:

- How long do you want to take paid, or unpaid, leave?
- When will you go back to work?
- What are your childcare options and what will they cost?
- What kind of infrastructure and safety net are you going to put in place so that you can return to work knowing your children will be well cared for?

That last part is a major question, as childcare costs continue to rise. If you're in a dual-income relationship, it's worth talking in advance and in depth with your partner about what makes the most sense until your child is school age. If your career has potential for significant growth, then investing in childcare or agreeing that your partner will take on primary childcare duties so you can advance in your job may make the most sense. Childcare is expensive, but if it allows your and your partner's careers to grow, it may well be worth it. And most parents only need full-time childcare until their children go to school.

WHAT ABOUT FREELANCERS AND GIG WORKERS?

Freelancers have always been around, and the gig economy continues to expand for millennials and Generation Z. Gig work has many pros and cons, and it's up to you to determine the cost-benefit analysis that works for you. (Or, if you don't have a choice, the best way to make it work.) My job is to help make your financial life as strong and healthy as possible regardless.

Almost everything I've written here also applies to freelance and gig workers. You might not have a permanent boss or coworkers, but you have supervisors you report to and clients you work with. You might not be eligible for a promotion, but you can go after jobs that pay better or have more responsibility. You might not get paid sick leave or have access to a corporate sponsored 401(k), but you can budget days off, set up a SEP IRA and solo 401(k), and start saving for your future.

If you're a freelancer, understanding the ideas laid out in this book will bolster your financial prospects and professional future as much or more than if you were a conventional employee. When you are an employee, your company provides a financial structure in the form of a regular paycheck and some degree of security. When you are self-employed, you must create that structure on your own, understanding the financial fundamentals, setting aside money every paycheck so you have a financial cushion, and creating financial security for yourself and on your own terms.

You don't have a boss to talk to, so my best advice is to recast yourself as your boss/the owner of a small business, where you're the business. A lot of people become their own boss because they don't want to work for someone else. But the money you earn is still going toward supporting yourself and people who are important to you, and you are still accountable to your clients. So, what kind of boss do you want to be? You get to pick. Do you want to be someone who is really organized, or are you a more seat-of-the-pants manager? Spend some time reflecting, considering, brainstorming. Without quarterly check-ins with a boss at a 9–5 job, what other structures could you put in place to keep yourself on track for success? How will you review your own strengths, weaknesses, and progress?

Regardless, you don't have to do this alone. Research and connect with groups that support the kind of work you do. You might also want to educate yourself about how unions work and see if there is one that makes sense for you. Many people in different kinds of work—actors, musicians, artists, writers—are freelancers, and many have unions that offer important benefits.

NEGOTIATING RATES AS A FREELANCER/GIG WORKER

One core component of successful freelancing is the ability to communicate knowledgeably and confidently with a wide variety of people. That includes engaging with your professional team about finances and with clients about contracts, fees, rates, and project scope—the equivalent of establishing your salary as an employee. You'll go through the same analysis we discussed in Chapter 3, with an additional layer: your income will be supporting not just your personal expenses but those of the business itself.

Rate negotiation is the equivalent of asking for a raise in a traditional work environment. It's one of your main tools as a freelancer. So even though it can be intimidating, it's imperative that you push through.

For help setting rates, I recommend forming a study group or joining an organization in your field. That will give you a set of people to ask key questions like, "Based on my experience, what would you charge?" If you're a podcaster, for example, you probably know other people who are podcasters. Tell them you're trying to put together a group to share ideas and strategies on how to better take care of ourselves financially and professionally. It's a bit like starting a financial book club (read the epilogue for more on that). And it can be a source of camaraderie, professional support, and even new business. Plus, that group should be able to help you establish a floor or benchmark for how you should be paid. You can ask them what they charge, tell them your education and background, and then do the math. (Many industries also use a standard multiplier that takes into account the desired hourly pay rate plus overhead to come up with a billing rate. Your peer group can help you find this standard.)

When you take on a new client, she will ask you your rate. Don't be afraid to ask for what you know you're worth. If she says, "I can't afford that," you can decide whether you want to negotiate and find a rate that works for both of you.

There are many reasons to be flexible: maybe you believe in the organization or cause, or you know working with this person or organization will give your reputation a boost. You may be going through a slow period and need money quickly. Every year I do a few pro bono speaking engagements, typically for schools. It gives me a way to refine new material as well as exposure to new audiences and people who will buy my books. Any reason you do this is valid, as long as you aren't accepting the lower rate because you think you don't have a choice. If a new client wants to negotiate a rate that will not work for you, you can always negotiate the scope of the work instead, or set an hours cap.

I also recommend you reevaluate your rates at least once a year; it's a worthy discipline to engage in regularly. Try, "It's a new year, and I wanted to let you know I'm raising my rates [X]%." Be prepared to explain why you are making this change. Your clients deserve to understand—even if the answer is that, like everyone else, you're trying to keep up with inflation.

> One piece of advice that a freelancer friend passed onto me for finding rates: take the amount that you would make as an annual salary at a full-time job and divide that by 1,000 for your hourly rate. (So, if you are a freelancer editor, for example, and you would be making $65,000 as a staff copy editor, you should charge $65 per hour, and so on.)
>
> She has used this tool for 20 years and swears by it. Clients sometimes push back, multiplying it by 40 hours a week and 52 weeks a year, and coming up with what seems to them an astronomical sum (though often about what they make annually!). She points out that she has overhead, health insurance costs, disability insurance costs, unpaid vacation time, and a retirement fund to pay for—and that when she works billable hours, she rarely works an eight-hour day, nor would they expect her to.
>
> If they keep protesting, she tells them, "I'm better educated than most lawyers, with more experience, and I work faster and better. But I'm *way* cheaper than any lawyer." That usually does the trick.

A WORD ABOUT BURNOUT (FOR EVERYONE)

Burnout has become an enormous problem among working adults. I'd like to take this opportunity to remind you, at the end of a chapter about work, that you are more than your job. With luck, you will also have conversations with your boss about work-life balance. You will find a way to take an interest in each other's outside lives, and you'll share a view that you are each a whole person with strengths and joys and goals who exists outside of the office, Zoom room, and email box.

If you can manage your relationships with your colleagues and boss well, you'll be able to reserve time for rest. You will take time off on weekends or to take a vacation when you need to—without feeling stress or guilt. If you're a gig worker, creating financial infrastructure can help you take days off and feel like you can afford it. If you're being paid a fair wage and advocating for yourself, you're probably living more manageably, with less stress about debt or bills.

But all of us need reminders to create space for ourselves. (I need to remind myself of this too!)

We deserve breaks! We deserve rest! We deserve to spend time with our friends, loved ones, partners! Managing our money well and making sure we are earning what we deserve can help make that happen.

CHAPTER NINE

BUILDING A FINANCIALLY SOUND MARRIAGE

I took my kids to see *Mary Poppins Returns* several years ago. The Banks household is in mourning because their mother has recently died. Then Michael Banks, now an adult with three children, learns that his house will be repossessed in five days unless he can pay back a loan. Just as all seems lost, Michael and his sister receive the surprise of a lifetime when Mary Poppins—the beloved nanny from their childhood—arrives to save the day.

I saw the original *Mary Poppins* as a kid and then again as an adult, when I was a mother working in finance. This time, my view of the family was new: I could see how wealthy and uptight they were. While Michael's father was a banker, I suspect Mr. Banks rarely had conversations about money with his children (except for the song about the value of a "tuppence"). Michael grew up intimidated by money. It becomes clear in the second movie that his late wife was the one who dealt with all their household finances. After her death, Michael is left unequipped to handle their financial life, with catastrophic consequences.

I couldn't help but watch the movie through a financial lens because I see this kind of thing happen *all the time*. As I watched, I saw a family in financial disarray. The father is in debt and will be on the street if he can't find a way to pay back the loan. He is grieving, ineffective, and poorly organized, and as the responsible parent, he's doing a pretty terrible job. The family has no emergency funds. The children can see the stress this is causing and feel powerless.

I tallied all the lessons to be learned: Teach your children financial fundamentals. Keep a list of where everything is, just in case. And *talk about money with your spouse.*

Considering the tensions many people experience around money, and the widespread fear of discussing it, it makes sense that many couples are happy to let the responsibility of money management fall on one person's shoulders, rather than going through the trouble of financial collaboration. I see it all the time. But I'd argue that a partnership can't reach its full potential without this kind of communication. Both practically and emotionally, relying on one person to take care of everything leads very frequently to disaster.

But whether you're 20 years old and in your first romantic relationship or 65 and married 40 years, you can craft a financial partnership that makes you happy and works for both of you.

MONEY MESSAGES

I worked recently with a woman named Sasha, whose father had been a successful business owner and the president of a company based in a small town. Even so, she had grown up living very frugally. Throughout her childhood, she heard her parents say, "Money doesn't grow on trees." For Sasha and her family, that meant always living beneath their means—and I mean way beneath. She continued that habit through a successful career in finance and a substantial inheritance from her parents.

While this family's approach may seem admirable, it really led to a life unlived. Because her parents were so conservative financially, Sasha's portfolio reflected that conservative message. She never felt she had enough and was literally afraid she would end up homeless. Although her joys were travel and fashion, and she could afford to indulge in both, she usually didn't. She loved being near the water, yet she was living in a desert valley.

One of our first steps was helping Sasha see that she could afford a home near the water. We also created a budget to help her *spend with joy* rather than guilt, but it took a full year of financial conversations about her dreams to begin to break down deep-seated money messages.

At first blush, Sasha's situation might not feel terribly applicable to your life and experiences. After all, most people aren't dealing with large inheritances. But that struggle to shake off old ideas about money cuts across class. Whether you have $10 million or $10,000, we can all learn from the root issue here: our ideas about money, many of which we picked up early in life, can stop us from living as richly (in the non-money sense) as we might and instead saddle us with fear or guilt or shame.

We all live with messages from our families, both implicit and explicit, about how money works and what it's for. These messages continue to affect us into adulthood. Some are mantras passed down in a family but also repeated in society. Here's a random list I've had clients recite to me over the years:

- Three topics are never to be discussed at the dinner table: money, politics, and religion.

- Daddy makes the money; Mother spends it.
- Never rely on a man to take care of you financially.
- Life is short. Don't save the good china—use it and enjoy it.
- If you have nothing to wish for, you might as well die.
- Always have your rainy-day fund.
- You can't take it with you!
- Money can't buy happiness.
- Waste not, want not.

Other messages may be unique to a particular family, or they may be ideas you've internalized about your habits and capacities:

- I've never had a head for numbers. They're just so confusing for me.
- We were really poor and never had enough. Now that I have money, I never feel comfortable spending it.
- We were the richest family in town, and we lived well, but my parents were always careful to appear modest about their wealth. We played it down, and I still feel guilty when I spend money.
- Give away as much as you can and enjoy the gift of being able to give. Your life will be richer.
- We were poor and had nothing. Now, I want the best of everything.
- I could die tomorrow; why save?
- I've got a great job. I'll always do well.

Whether or not you talked openly about money in your family, all of us have absorbed messages from home. Some families have less money and end up passing on messages of shame. Some families have lots of money and are afraid they will disincentivize their kids to work if they "give them too much"—and, as a result, behave in a way that is withholding and ungenerous. Either way, these messages can create confusion and build resentment. I've seen them hurt both individuals and families.

YOU AND YOUR MONEY

You know that saying, that in order to build a healthy relationship with somebody else, first you have to love yourself? There's a corollary in personal finance. How can you talk to your partner about "what's important to us" if you don't know what's important to *you*? Before you have a healthy relationship with your partner about money, you have to get straight with yourself.

Your first step is identifying what your money messages are, without judgment. Whether you grew up with more money than you needed or not enough, those messages you internalized will impact how you earn, spend, save, and invest it in your own life. Some of these are positive, creating joy and a sense of empowerment. Many are defeatist, breeding guilt and secrecy.

Spend some time brainstorming all the things you remember your parents, siblings, or other family members telling you about money. Then, reflect on how those messages affect your spending and saving habits. What conversations stress you out? What ways of spending money make you happy? Write it all down.

> In the appendix, I've included surveys on four topics: Life Transitions, Financial Life Transitions, Family Life Transitions, and Legacy Life Transitions, all developed by Carol Anderson, founder of Money Quotient.
>
> All are effective tools that will help you figure out where you are now and where you want to go when it comes to money.

Don't forget that money messages aren't always explicit. You were also taught by example. One way to identify these more implicit messages is to think about how your family spent money when you were young—and how they didn't. Some families would not dream of buying a new car and are generally thrifty, but they eat at expensive restaurants every month. Some buy expensive cars and clothes but don't have passports because they are less interested in traveling internationally. These are money messages, too, and a way to teach values. (If your parents are still alive, consider asking them about this; it can lead to some beautiful conversations.)

Lastly, I'll add this: almost everyone comes from a mindset of either abundance or scarcity, whether they recognize it or not. Stephen Covey coined these terms in his best-selling book, *The 7 Habits of Highly Effective People*. "Scarcity mentality" refers to a kind of zero-sum thinking; people in this mode might view resources as a finite pie, so that if one party takes a big piece, less remains for everyone else. This feeling of scarcity can cause what psychologists call "tunneling," or ignoring other needs and obligations to focus on a scarce resource.

Conversely, an abundance mentality suggests a different paradigm: that there are enough resources for everybody. Practicing seeing where you have abundance can help you broaden your perspective, solve problems, and make decisions that will benefit you long term—even when your resources are low. A mindset of abundance can help you see the world as full of opportunities and makes it easier to share.

These mindsets don't necessarily have anything to do with how much money you actually have. It's more about how you *feel* about what you have. There are plenty of rich people who worry about having enough and plenty of people who have less and think, "I'll be fine." Spend some time considering which side you tend to land on. Knowing this about yourself will help you talk to your partner about where you're coming from, since this way of thinking can affect many aspects of your relationship with money—from how you two set up individual and joint bank accounts to whether or when you fight about bills.

It's okay if it's a struggle to stay in abundance: I get it. Personally and professionally, I'm surrounded by so much of other people's wealth that I sometimes have to remind myself that I'm doing okay and I'm happy with what I have.

Some days it's easier to remember than others. It's a process and a practice! But it's also just a nicer place to live, and it helps you cultivate generosity too.

Now, before we move on, take a breath. If this is the first time you're being honest with yourself about your money messages, this might take some time to sink in. The goal here is to identify the money messages you grew up with. Then, figure out which messages no longer serve you and which messages you want to keep. Make space and time for that. You're learning important things about yourself.

STARTING THE MONEY CONVERSATION WITH YOUR PARTNER

There's a reason people don't talk to their nearest and dearest about money. If you grew up in a frugal household and your partner grew up in a less frugal one, your spending patterns are likely to be different. The differing money messages you received may create conflict. This is a reality worth acknowledging. We haven't been given the tools to comfortably have these sometimes-tricky discussions. However, these conversations are not just possible—they're essential.

If your spouse or life partner has always been the one to handle the finances, and you've never talked about money together before, these first conversations might be met with confusion, hostility, or suspicion. That's normal. Last fall, Paloma came to me because she had no idea how much she and her husband had saved for retirement. She was anxious because her husband kept putting her off whenever she asked about it. His first response was, "Why the sudden interest?" Other reactions that have been shared with me include: "You wouldn't know what I was talking about anyway," "Why do you want to know now, after all these years?" and "Don't you trust me?"

Paloma and I practiced follow-ups together, which helped prepare her to field her husband's evasive responses. Here are some possibilities for phrasing that might help you:

- "I'm asking because I'd like to understand our finances better. You've done all the work for a long time, and I'd like to help share the responsibility."
- "We're partners in so many other ways; I'd love to learn more about what's going on financially."
- "You've done a really great job, and I appreciate everything you've done so far. And I think it's important that I start to understand what our finances look like too."

Even though this person loves you, a change in dynamic like this can feel disorienting. With this in mind, you can approach this conversation in a way that's not threatening. Acknowledging the real work they've put in is important but so is asserting your right to information. Try something like, "I'm sure you recognize that part of doing a good job is making sure I understand what's going on."

As you and your partner begin your money discussions, if you find the subject causes a great deal of tension or anxiety, you might consider bringing the topic up in premarital or couple's counseling—or engaging a financial advisor or money coach. The internet is full of great resources for you. But if you don't do anything else, my go-to technique is making time for "Money Dates."

A DIFFERENT KIND OF DATE NIGHT

You don't have to be married or in a long-term partnership to have great money conversations with the person you love. I love to recommend the practice of going on "Money Dates" to my clients. At its core, a Money Date is a structured financial check-in that you build around something fun. Go for a hike and talk as you walk along. Find a cafe and have a cup of coffee and some double chocolate cake. Cook brunch and chat comfortably in your kitchen. The only timing I discourage is holding Money Dates after work, since people are often tired, and their blood sugar is low. That also means it's a bad idea to meet on an empty stomach. Weekend mornings after breakfast or early afternoons often work well, after a good night's sleep.

Treat your first Money Date like an orientation to each other's financial worlds. One good way to start is to each separately fill out the Money Quotient "Financial Life Transitions" in the Appendix. This survey asks about transitions in 12 financial categories—for example, income, spending habits, or level of debt.

Spend half an hour talking about a few of the points of agreement or similarity in your surveys. Don't fight about anything; just share. If you check that you are anticipating something long-term and your partner circles short-term, that's a conversation starter. This also might be a good time to share your money messages. (You might consider jotting some down before you begin so they're fresh in your mind.) From there, you might discuss how your families managed debt or savings, or how they decided what was worth spending money on.

Don't feel you need to cover everything on your first Money Date! This is an ice breaker, and it's important that it's a good experience, not stressful or exhausting.

Make sure to end on a positive note, with your tasty treat or some flowers you found on your walk; a reward mechanism will ensure your new habit continues. And before you finish, schedule your next Money Date. Talk together about what cadence might be best for you. I suggest starting with once a month.

What you cover at your next meeting is up to you. The idea behind Money Dates is to set aside time to tackle money issues and build your financial life together. You might consider delving more into your money backgrounds. Your early Money Dates are also great for establishing shared goals, which are key to navigating your financial differences. Maybe your partner didn't grow up with much and is now making a lot of money and wants to spend it, but you grew up in a frugal household and spending money feels uncomfortable. If you're saving for a house or car, and your partner is meeting his obligations toward your shared goal, that's going to help you feel a lot more comfortable with their choices. Acknowledging your differences and establishing goals together is a good way to begin, making space for you to work toward the future both of you are hoping for. Start a list of future topics and goals. Feel free to revise and add to your list as your financial lives evolve.

Eventually, your dates will become less about negotiation and more about updating each other on what's happening in your financial lives. "I bought that stock we talked about, and this is how it's performing" perhaps, or "I've been at my job for a year now, and they're going to match my 401(k). How much should I put in, and how should we invest that money?" If neither of you knows the answer, maybe you'll talk about hiring a financial advisor or reading some articles on financial management. Maybe you'll go look at the Schwab website about 401(k) best practices, and your partner will check out what Fidelity says about retirement planning—then report back to each other while sharing a smoothie, a slice of cheesecake, or a martini.

Ultimately, making time for Money Dates means making time for you as a team. You can start to ask, "What do we want to learn about each other? What information do we need to share? How do we need to educate ourselves?"

It's a practice that can follow you your whole life. I know from experience! My husband and I have been devotees of Money Dates for decades. Some years, we were facing unexpected cutbacks and had to talk about what to spend less on. I would promise not to buy another piece of clothing above a certain agreed price for the next six months; he would agree not to spend more on wine. We would end the meeting feeling as though we were really in the trenches together, closer than ever.

SEPARATE PROPERTY VERSUS COMMUNITY PROPERTY

"Separate" and "community" property are legal terms that refer to how assets (and debts!) are divided in a marriage. In California, where I lived for many years, property acquired by either spouse during a marriage is considered "community" property—also sometimes known as "marital" property or "joint" property—and it belongs equally to both partners of the marriage. Separate property is typically money you earned before entering the relationship that you want to keep separate. It can also include property acquired as a gift or through inheritance at any time. But every state is different. Make sure to speak with a lawyer for specifics as they apply to you.

Some couples opt to sign a "separate property agreement" that specifies that certain assets remain independent from the marriage, sort of like a prenuptial agreement. In some states, this kind of agreement is unnecessary because the law dictates this separation for you. In others, unless you create this legal framework, everything you own becomes communal after marriage. Note that that often includes debt too. If you incur $100,000 dollars in debt during the marriage, your spouse may be legally obligated to repay it—even if you contracted for the loan in your sole name. And vice versa!

If you're considering marriage, it's a good idea to understand the laws that define separate property in your state. And if you have money you earned before marriage that you want to keep separate, it's important not to commingle your assets. Keep that money in a bank account apart from any communal property and be careful not to use it for joint things that might make the boundaries muddy. (Also note that if you're getting or contemplating getting divorced, and your spouse suggests moving to a different state, it's worth looking into what that state's laws are before you agree.)

Just like the conversation about money messages, talking about separate and community property and how you want to divide your assets as you move forward in your relationship together can be sensitive. Even in the best partnerships, this kind of discussion can provoke defensiveness: "What's the matter? Are you worried we're going to get divorced? Don't you trust me?" It's worth acknowledging that even the most supportive partner may have some feelings about this.

All these conversations are improved when you approach them with empathy and compassion. Acknowledge that both of you are working outside your comfort zones and that it is a mark of how much you care about the relationship that you're willing to "go there" to engage. Being a team means that if one of you is more comfortable talking about these difficult things, part of your job is to help your counterpart get comfortable too.

In the end, you're in partnership with this person. If you can't have these kinds of conversations, it may raise a red flag about other difficult conversations you'll inevitably have over the course of your years together.

YOURS, MINE, AND OURS

You won't be surprised to hear that I don't believe there is any one *right way* to share finances. What's important is that you work together, that you each feel safe to suggest and make choices, and that you both feel comfortable with your shared and individual goals.

Until fairly recently, the institution of marriage was mostly about forging a financial partnership and deepening familial alliances. That's why women had dowries, right? Women's value was in our dowries, and that mindset often impacted the marriage too. My point is twofold. First, we've come a long way. Today, fortunately, we're in a place where marriage can be so much more than that, truly a partnership.

But looking back at how far we've come also means understanding that it's taken a lot of evolution and growth to get here. If it's a struggle to make your marriage feel like that true partnership when it comes to finances, don't beat yourself up about it. My intent here is to describe how things *can* be and to highlight that you now have an option that didn't exist before.

All that leads me to the most common question I get about managing family finances: separate or joint accounts? While I deeply believe everyone needs to have their own independent account under their own sole control, I also believe there is no "right way" beyond that.

Still, I'll say that I do tend to favor a setup where each person has an individual account while also contributing to a joint account. In this system, you decide together which bills will be paid jointly and set aside funds from each paycheck for the joint account. (Direct deposit is an ideal way to make sure this gets done smoothly every month.) Some couples decide that one person will pay all the utility bills, while the primary breadwinner may pay the rent or mortgage. There's no rule here; these are just guidelines. You're doing it right as long as it feels fair to both of you.

I also recommend that if you and your partner make different amounts of money, you calculate how much each person pays by percentage. If one of you makes three times more than the other, for example, then the one making more would deposit three times more money into the joint account; if that person is making double, then twice as much, and so on.

That also goes for figuring out your budget as a couple. Let's say you make about $60,000 a year, and your partner makes about $80,000. The general rule of thumb is that no more than 25–30% of your gross pay should go toward rent or mortgage. If your monthly salary is $5,000 a month, that means your maximum is $1,250. If your partner makes $7,000 a month, that's $1,750. So, *combined,* you can afford to pay $3,000 in rent. But your own portion is still going to be $1,250. That's equitable; that's what *you* can afford.

Even once you figure out your system, don't assume that what's equitable will stay that way. This is a dynamic process. If one of you gets promoted, or one of you gets laid off, then the math changes. And the chances of one of you getting laid off over the course of your lives is pretty high. (I, too, have been laid off!)

Talk through how you might support each other if one of you is out of work—before the actual emergency happens. Will you have one emergency fund or two? How will you handle it if it's a small layoff, or if 16,000 other people lose their jobs at the same time? Ask yourselves how you feel about the idea of supporting each other between gigs. Your partner might say, "I don't have a problem at all." Or maybe, "I could do it for six months, but then it would be really hard," or "I'd still like you to pay a part of our bills, but I can take on an extra chunk." No one is being contentious, just honest. Talking about it beforehand allows you to negotiate without the urgency and emotion that comes up when someone loses a job.

Ultimately, you want a system that will allow you to have frank discussions about equity and independence. The Money Date structure can help navigate these discussions well. It was important to me (and I suspect it might be important to you) to partner with someone who isn't threatened by sharing the financial workload. As women increasingly dominate in college and are paid more afterward, this is becoming an issue. But I am not ashamed of the money I make. You shouldn't be either.

BUDGET VERSUS ALLOWANCE

It's not unusual to have an allowance when you're young. Culturally, in the United States, it was also common practice in the mid-twentieth century for husbands to give their wives allowances to manage the family budget. There are also cultures where the husband hands over his paycheck to his wife, and she gives *him* an allowance for commuting costs, lunch, and pocket money. She pays all the bills and manages the money, then hands her husband his weekly envelope of spending money.

I won't come out against allowances all the way, because—as in the manner just described—in some cases they basically serve as a budget for spending a given amount of money in a given way. If you and your partner have done the work, your financial values are aligned, and you've decided it's the way you are going to manage things, it can make sense. But I'd still rather call it something else. For me, giving an adult an "allowance" feels controlling and patronizing. Could you call it an "allocation"? Part of your budgeting process? That way, you have a set amount to spend, and no one is "giving" or "allowing" it to anyone else.

Another strategy is to agree on a spending limit that merits a check-in. For example, you agree to talk to each other before spending more than a certain amount on an item or expense. Speaking from my perspective, I don't ever want to have to ask my husband for permission to buy, for example, a nice coat. But we regularly discuss and ask for input when considering an expensive purchase. One of us will say, "I'm thinking of buying [X expensive thing]; what do you think?"

His response might be, "What are the pros and cons?"

Then perhaps we'll talk through my motivation for the purchase and possible drawbacks. I might conclude, "Having thought about it, I'll hold off," to "I totally hear you. I may still buy the item, but I'll pay for it out of my own funds."

Ultimately, this is about agency. You each want to make your own decisions about how to meet your needs and wants. However, you are still part of a partnership. Just because you recognize your own agency doesn't mean you can't respect the other person's as well.

As you consider all this, I recommend these additional best practices:

- Just as everyone should have their own bank account, everyone should have their own credit card. Having a credit card in your name gives you the opportunity to build your own credit score. It's an important component of your independence.
- I recommend sharing no more than two joint credit cards (just as I do with individual cards), since too many cards can become confusing and out of control.
- Keep it simple, even with equity. Even as I wholeheartedly endorse equitably dividing your expenses, I also advise against getting too carried away with this kind of math. If you start making all kinds of expenses proportional, that opens up opportunities for fights about how different resources get used within your relationship, which discourages empathy or generosity between you. Fighting about things like how much you eat or whether you turn off the lights when you leave a room does not make for a healthy relationship.

THE IMPORTANCE OF TRANSPARENCY

That brings me to my last point. As you build your new financial structure as a couple, prioritize creating a culture of transparency and trust. Most people don't like surprises, especially negative ones. I've shepherded clients as they dealt with mountains of debt that a loved one left behind and that no one knew about. I've worked with clients whose husbands were supporting their in-laws without saying so. Some people—you would be surprised how common this is—buy a bunch of stuff, keep it in the trunk of their car, and smuggle it up to the closet when the spouse isn't around. If you're going to build a healthy relationship with money and your partner, that is the *opposite* of what we're going for.

If you're up front about a major purchase and discuss it in advance, that gives your partner an opportunity to push back, and that can be uncomfortable. Your partner might say, "Wait a second, that sounds kind of expensive. Can we really afford it?"

But if you've done your homework, you'll be able to respond: Yes, *we* can. Or you'll be able to advocate for yourself and say, "It might be a stretch for us, but it's meaningful to me." Suddenly the decision becomes a *we* thing versus a *you* thing.

These moments of disagreement are also opportunities to better understand each other. If your partner disagrees with something you want to spend money on, ask why. What about the expense makes him uncomfortable? What is she afraid of? Often, when we talk about spending money, we're making *value judgments*. What does it say, for example, if a person is willing to spend more on organic fruits and vegetables, international travel, or charitable giving? Learning about each other's values is another form of intimacy. You're spending your life with—and maybe even creating life with—this person. This is just another way to understand each other more fully.

CHAPTER TEN

RAISING MONEY-CONFIDENT KIDS

I was lucky to grow up in a family that was comfortable talking about money. As a young adult, I was aware of how much money my dad made. I knew where my parents had to economize. I received an allowance starting quite early and had a bank account to put that allowance in. At first, of course, it was maybe a quarter a week. Even then, I remember thinking, "What can I do with *that*?" (That's one of the reasons I started selling Christmas cards door to door at nine years old: to have more of my own money. My parents were skeptical but ultimately supportive.)

In a lot of ways, our family was a typical Midwestern, middle-class family. Both my parents grew up during the Depression and WWII and were fairly frugal. They were conscious about how they chose to spend their money and often talked about where they decided to save and how they did it. Rather than sitting down and showing me how to make a budget, their approach was to give me a hands-on education as they lived their financial lives. For example, a large bakery near our house sold day-old bread and baked goods at a discount, so we would buy our bread there. After all, my father said, we'd save a few bucks. Other days, I'd laugh when he drove across town to buy the cheapest gas. He'd counter that he'd organized his errands in that area so that he could fill his tank there.

I know some people are not as lucky as I was. Many of my clients grew up in homes where they were taught not to talk about sex, politics, ... or money. But one of the core duties we parents sign up for is helping our kids build essential money communication skills and financial management so they can discern how and where to spend and talk about their money.

In addition to my work as a financial professional, I teach workshops on personal finance, most often for teenagers, college students, and young people who are just starting to move into the adult world. These classes cover the financial fundamentals, including what I like to refer to as "BIRDS": budgeting, investments, retirement, debt, and savings—in short, the first few chapters of this book. I add other topics depending on the age group. And as we go, I'm always conscious that in the workshops I am modeling how to talk naturally about money.

With older high school kids, once we've covered the five fundamentals, their next questions are usually: "How do I get a credit card? When I graduate from high school or college, what should I do first?" The college kids want to know about building credit scores, buying a car, and maybe saving up to backpack through Europe. And recent graduates have often not thought about what life will cost them beyond rent, so we talk about utilities, food, and first and last deposits on apartments. If they're a little older and entering the workforce, we map out budgets and salary requirements and talk about 401(k)s and retirement savings.

So often, these kids tell me the class is transformative for them. Not because what I'm telling them is so magical, but because it just never even occurred to them to sit down and figure out what their expenses could be. They may have had vague ideas about the cost of living or retirement but have not been clear on the specifics. The workshop helps them see exactly what life costs and how far their first paycheck may (or may not) get them. They leave the class maybe a little daunted by the demands of adulthood but also more confident that they have the skills to manage it.

What is so crucial about all this, what I want you to take away from my description here, is that these are all bright kids: smart, hardworking, high achieving. But they often *have no idea how to do it on their own.* That's what this chapter is about: raising kids who are savvy about money—who understand its value, how to talk about it, and how to use it consciously and carefully as a tool toward happiness and fulfillment.

As your kids grow from babies into young adults, the idea of teaching them about personal finance soon mushrooms from allowance, chores, and savings accounts, to balancing a checkbook, paying with credit cards, using a debit card, and paying off student loans. When does it start? When *should* it start? When does it end? How can you talk about these topics when you're not sure how to think about them yourself? Let's dive in.

CULTIVATING A MONEY-CONFIDENT HOME

The prospect of preparing your children to navigate the complexities of the financial world can be daunting. The good news is that the first step is also the least complicated. Just start talking. Create an environment where you can share information, views, and values in bite-size portions, and where your kids feel comfortable asking you questions so that they can build their financial knowledge bit by bit. Establishing a money-confident atmosphere will help your kids get comfortable with the topic, develop skills around how to talk about it, learn to find answers to their money questions, and gain important background on how their own family handles money. And all of that will be especially useful, of course, once they leave home and begin their own financial adventures.

Some of this process is specific and concrete: carving out time to talk about financial concepts, taking your kids on grocery store field trips, and helping them start a savings account. I also recommend keeping track of terms your kids hear on the radio or see online or on TV: *stock market, stock equity, bonds,* etc. Keep a list on the fridge or a bulletin board and define them together as you go, without worrying too much about what sticks. The terms are secondary to the atmosphere you're creating. What's more important is letting your kids know that there are no dumb questions and that you can find the answers together.

Your list might also include terms that aren't factual but are still key to talking about money in our society. One example is "rich versus poor." Your kids will ask you about the difference at some point as they start to hear these words used around them—most often in the context of "Are we rich?" or "Are we poor?" I always like to start by engaging them about what they've picked up so far on the subject. Ask, "What does that word mean to you?" After all, if they're asking, it means they have some concept of the idea already.

FAMILY VALUES

The rest of the work happens in conversational chunks at unexpected times during your daily life and throughout your kids' childhood and adolescence. These conversations can start when your kids are three or four years old, as they start to ask you to buy things for them.

Look at the moment your son asks you to buy him a book or toy as an opportunity. You might say, "Oh, honey, we use money to pay for that," or "You have two of those. If you want another one, maybe you should give one to your cousin." Just starting to connect these concepts—that the things we want cost money and that making choices about how you spend your money is worth doing—will plant the seeds for future growth. If you think about it, what you're really doing is starting a conversation about your values. What do you want to teach your kids about what's worth saving for and splurging on? What do you want to teach them about charity or discipline?

Once your kids start going to birthday parties, they may see some of their friends with petting zoos or fancy gift bags. (Sure, petting zoos may seem over the top, but fancy is relative. Every family makes different choices based on what they value.) They may notice from the school bus that some of their friends live in smaller and even run-down houses. They'll go to playdates and see some kids dressed in different kinds of clothes or eating different foods. Children notice all that stuff. You'll start to get questions based on their observations: "Why does Karim have a pool, but we don't?" "Why doesn't Steven's house have an upstairs?" "Why does David live in a house, but we live in an apartment building?"

The real content of these questions often has nothing to do with money. It's what's *behind* the money, what the money *means*, that they're picking up on. So, the first response to all these questions is, "Why do you ask?" Take the time to unpack them a little, using the questions as a jumping-off point to discuss family values, family history, and family goals.

Take the pool example. You might ask your daughter, "Why do you think it's important to Karim's family to have a pool?"

"Well, his mom likes to swim every day," she might say.

So, you respond, "Well, that seems like a pretty good reason to have a pool. Does anyone in our family want to swim every day?"

"Not really."

"Well, that's one reason we don't have a pool."

The message you want to send here—and the one I'm sending to you—is that discussions about money involve *judgment* but do not have to be *judgmental*. Maybe Karim's family life really revolves around swimming.

Maybe both parents use the pool for exercise; maybe they have regular pool parties with their friends or their kids' friends. Maybe they've made other sacrifices or choices so that they can have a pool, a tennis court, or a fancy car. One thing I've learned about working in wealth management is that people make all kinds of choices around the stuff that is important to them. Then they decide not to spend money somewhere else so they can balance out that decision.

These conversations are an opportunity to share your values and priorities. Maybe you'd rather bring lunch to work every day, saving money so you can spend it on experiences: theater, travel, dining out. Maybe you prefer to buy second-hand clothes because it's better for your budget and in line with your values about sustainability. Or maybe your idea of sustainability is spending more on a well-made, high-quality coat that you will wear for 20 years.

I particularly encourage you to be deliberate about the messages you're sending your kids around generosity. As you move through the world with them, are you teaching them that it's a place of abundance or scarcity? Are you encouraging them to think creatively about resources? Are you praising expressions of gratitude and impulses to give gifts? Are you showing them how the ways they spend their money might affect other people? And are you discussing the difference between being frugal and being cheap?

In my mind, the difference lies in considering how money choices may impact someone else. If you're happy eating a PBJ for lunch, that's being frugal, which is your choice. But if you're feeding someone else, generosity might be more important than frugality. When you go out to dinner and you split a meal with your friend or your spouse, that's being frugal. But not tipping the waiter or tipping 10%—that's being cheap. (Tipping is a particularly great context for teaching your children about generosity; you can show them how the way you tip a waiter can make or ruin their day, with the difference of just a few dollars on your end.)

Helping your kids differentiate between "frugal" and "cheap" will help them understand the power of making choices about money and develop sensitivities that will matter to friends who have less. I try to both tell and show my kids that generosity is about greater awareness for how we're all connected. In friendship, generosity might mean giving thoughtful gifts or being gracious with your time and energy. In a community, it might mean finding ways big and small to give to charity. In a workplace, generosity might translate to ample sick leave. What are you showing your kids about how to put generosity into action? What might you be showing them accidentally when you think they're not looking?

RAISING GROUNDED CHILDREN

Many well-to-do people worry about raising kids who won't take their family's money for granted. They want instead to instill values of generosity, hard work, thoughtfulness, and compassion—in short, for their children to remain grounded.

When clients ask me about this, my initial answer is always that if you're asking the question, that's a good start. But, of course, there's more to say.

1. Follow the middle path.
    We all know people who have a lot of money and live a very rich life in material goods: big houses, fancy things. Parents who grew up with less often want to make sure their children have the best of everything, but that can backfire. Does that really reflect your values? Just because you can afford for the family to travel first class doesn't mean it's always the best decision. Maybe you prefer the five-star hotel, but do you need to get a suite every time? If you want to raise

grounded children, display grounded values. It doesn't make sense to spend money on things that aren't important to you just because you have it available—and your kids will notice if you do.

At the same time, though, Warren Buffet's late business partner, Charlie Munger, was known for giving this good advice: Don't make your kids go through unnecessary hardship; they'll just hate you for it. You don't need to live a less-than life just because you're trying to convey a message.

So, strive for that middle path and always return to your values. The idea that you should spend money (or not) in ways that reflect your values can be a guiding star in your efforts to raise grounded children. And having money shouldn't absolve your kids of their obligations to their community. You might help them get summer jobs or direct them to shovel the neighbor's driveway after a snowfall, to help them understand what it means to be a good neighbor and show them all the ways we need and help each other in a community.

I know for sure that your kids will remember what you do much more than what you say. If you talk about and believe that being involved in your community matters to you and your family, are you showing your kids what it looks like to volunteer and give to charity? If you support environmental causes, are you driving a Prius, even though you can afford a premium car?

2. Teach them to read the room.

Another important lesson to teach your kids is how to keep from accidentally showing off. Kids understand gradations of class and wealth better than anyone else; you're kidding yourself if you think they're in the dark about it.

Make sure to positively reinforce any sensitivity they show to others in this arena. Being respectful of your audience is a life skill just like any other. Teach them about status symbols: visible brand names, expensive fads, and even over-the-top generosity that may not have intrinsic value. And help them think through what pursuing those symbols will mean for their relationships. If they want the latest status coat, ask them: "If we get you that coat, how will other people react? How will they feel?" Help them see when indulgence or ostentation may make someone else feel less than; none of us want to do that to our friends. (This is also a good time to look at your own relationships. Is there anyone in your life you might be enacting this dynamic with and not noticing?)

3. Uncouple money and morals.

    Kids are obsessed with the "why" in everything, including money matters. Once yours notice that different people or families have more or less money, they'll start to ask you about it. Your job is to examine and deconstruct any assumptions they're making about why someone might have less money than you do, especially having to do with laziness or morality.

    Guide them through other possible explanations for why someone else might have less. Maybe your family has inherited wealth and this person doesn't; maybe this person prioritized a career they love but is less lucrative. Maybe this person got different money messages growing up. Point out that your kids are probably not going to be the richest or poorest in the room wherever they go—would they want someone who's richer to look down on them because they have less money? And emphasize that greater wealth does not necessarily equate to better character or values.

ALLOWANCE SYSTEMS

Even if you aren't worried about your kids staying grounded in the face of wealth, I'm sure you want them to have lots of practice thinking about and managing it—which brings us to allowance. My friend Leah used a system similar to the one my husband and I employed in our family. She started her kids with $1 a week for every year of age, from about five years old. There were some guidelines to go along with this money. She suggested her kids save between a quarter and half of their allowance for some future purchase or goal and that they give about 10% away to some sort of charity. But it wasn't mandatory.

What *was* mandatory was doing chores: taking out the garbage, doing their own laundry, making their beds, and making and packing their lunches and snacks. These tasks were not tied to their allowance. Leah and her husband, David, made clear that their kids had to do chores because they were part of the family unit. As part of the team, they were expected to contribute to the running of the household.

Leah and David used allowance as a teaching tool. (An allowance is a great way to help your kids develop money muscles as they grow older and as the allowance increases.) It paid for bus fare to school and around town, plus the occasional lunch out. The kids could use their extra money to buy something they wanted that Leah and David did not want to pay for. If the kids wanted an upgrade to fancier sneakers, they could use their allowance for the more expensive brand. They could take a Lyft instead of the bus. They could pack their lunch every day or could choose to spend their money on a deli sandwich. Allowance was a way for Leah and David not to have to provide money for the small things that their kids could navigate. And as the kids got older, they got more allowance, allowing them to make bigger decisions. It was a way for them to start to understand for themselves why it might be a good idea to save, invest, or share with others.

And Leah learned a few things too, lessons that I'm guessing most parents will recognize. When her daughter came to her asking for Air Jordan sneakers, she suggested two options. She would pay for an ordinary pair of shoes at the going rate. Her daughter could either pay for the difference in price with her allowance—or they could split the difference and add an extra chore. The sneakers suddenly didn't feel so necessary. (Not a bad way to deflect whining and negotiating at the shoe store.)

She also made sure to be clear from the start what purchases did and didn't need to come out of the allowance. If you're doing something similar, these items can be whatever you want—the ice cream store, for example, or lunches outside school. It could be *these* kinds of clothes (warm coat, school clothes, "Sunday" outfit, etc.) but not *those* (one more pair of stylish jeans, yet another cute summer dress). The system is inherently moldable to your needs and values and the needs of your kids. That's what's so great about it!

If you have multiple children, people often think treating kids equally is fair, but Leah found that fairness often meant spending time and money differently on each kid because each kid is unique. As the person who knows your child best, it's up to you to think about what they stand to gain from a paying job, a higher allowance, or some combination of work and pocket money. You also might spend a dinner conversation letting your kids know that you would underwrite a volunteer job or supplement an unpaid summer internship if it will lead to meaningful future work or build a résumé. (Thankfully, though, more internships are paid today, and many schools offer a stipend if the opportunity is unpaid.)

For example, from a young age my son has been an entrepreneur. From his first lemonade stand, he has long enjoyed creating small, and then not so small, business opportunities for himself. Meanwhile, my daughter (his twin) spent a lot of time volunteering. Both of them were building valuable skills. Should their allowances have been equal? Maybe in another family, yes. Ultimately, because my daughter wasn't working for a paycheck, she negotiated a higher allowance. I told my son that if he needed more, we could discuss it, but I didn't automatically match his to hers. After considering the other areas where we help him out, like new tires for his car, he decided he didn't need a higher allowance.

Understanding money trade-offs is pivotal for your kids. As I've written elsewhere, when I was a teenager, I held down multiple jobs to help pay the tuition for my high school and save for college. When I wanted to learn to ski, I earned money for lessons on the slope. If I hadn't had to work for a paycheck, could I have taken an internship, acted in more school plays, or otherwise enhanced my high school experience? Perhaps. But I learned a lot about teamwork by working at McDonald's. If your kid is earning either for pocket money or to help the family pay bills, make sure to reinforce that that's a valid way to spend time, too.

"WE CAN'T AFFORD IT"

Even with allowance in the mix, there will be a time when your child asks you to buy them something—a doll, a pair of sneakers, a ticket for a sports event, a car, whatever—and you feel it's beyond your limits. These "we can't afford it" moments happen to everyone, so let's be clear. They are not about some mistake you made in your life choices. They are not a reflection of your moral values or professional success. And they are not representative of a failure on your part. It's important that you remember that—and convey it to your kids.

Sometimes you have more money; sometimes you have less. You or a loved one might have had a sudden health emergency that wiped out your emergency fund. You might have gotten laid off. You might have invested a lot of money in a big stock, and suddenly it went down 70%. You might have a great job, but your bonus was lower than expected. I believe in being open with your children when money is tight.

You can still shield them from whatever anxieties you have about paying the bills. (Financial stress is a lot to put on a kid.) But it's absolutely okay to be frank about the facts. That includes walking them through your thinking. Here's why we aren't buying this thing; we could maybe swing it, but then we won't have money for anything else you want. Explaining this "choice" thought process will help them grasp the limitations of money, a hard but important idea. You might also remind them what's possible even with limited funds: a trip out to the skating rink or to the park, or a thoughtful but less expensive treat. (The best gift I got recently was homemade candied oranges from a friend who knows we like craft cocktails!)

The "we can't afford it" conversation also presents an opportunity to revisit those values you've been working to instill, especially if your denial is followed by the classic, "But Allie's parents got her one!" Again, keep the conversation away from judgment. Ask, "Why do you want that [jacket/toy/tech gadget]? If it's because Allie has one, do you want everything Allie has? Why is [X thing] important to you?" And remember that just because it's not a priority for *you* doesn't mean it's not one for your kid. Validate their desires and normalize any negative feelings. It's okay for them to be disappointed; it's okay for them to feel something is unfair.

DEBIT AND CREDIT CARDS

Another friend, Erin, who feels just as passionately about political activism as I do, always took her kids into the voting booth with her when they were young. Over the years, she used that same impulse to bring her kids to the bank to watch her deposit money, speak to the bank manager, or visit her safety deposit box. She wanted her children to start to feel comfortable accessing banking services at a young age, to understand that they had the right to be at the bank, to know how to navigate it, and to feel confident asking questions of the staff when they didn't. Even though it's more common now to do many of those tasks over the phone or online, she still tried to make a point of talking about how she was executing those tasks in the moment.

For the first several years of allowance, Erin and her wife, Delia, always did their best to pay their kids every week. The problem was, Erin was terrible at keeping cash on hand and always paid them late. Finally, when they were about 10 years old, Erin brought them to the bank to open accounts for them. She set up her account so that their allowance was transferred into her kids' accounts weekly. They each received debit cards, and she and Delia used the opportunity to teach them how those debit cards worked and how to keep track of the balance.

The amounts in each account were relatively small, so Erin asked the bank to waive the fees for each of the new bank accounts; since the accounts were tied to hers, the bank agreed. That also meant she could monitor their spending money and reimburse them via transfers for items she'd agreed that she'd pay for.

Plus, the debit cards gave Erin's kids a way to buy things online and a chance to start learning how to manage their spending on a slightly more sophisticated level. Once they were older and got the hang of a debit card, she added a credit card. This helped them learn to track credit card payments, or pay a card off entirely, and provided a way to begin building a credit score.

As we become an increasingly cashless society, managing a credit card is an especially fundamental skill. I recommend positioning credit cards as important tools that can be powerful when used well.

While it sounds a little ambiguous, I suggest that the right time for your kid to get a credit card is when they're ready. By that, I mean that credit cards are a grown-up tool for people with grown-up needs and who can talk about those needs in a grown-up way. Whereas you might make unilateral decisions as a parent when it comes to allowance or bank accounts, credit cards can be more of a family conversation. When we brought the possibility up with our teenagers, for example, our son was interested and wanted to learn more. Our daughter's reaction was, "Hmm, I don't know, that seems complicated." We still talked about the concept of credit and the complexities of credit reports and credit scores and how credit cards can be a useful tool. They didn't both need to be ready at the same time.

And now, as young adults, they both use their credit cards confidently and responsibly.

When your child is ready, you can help them apply. It used to be that when kids went to college, they were inundated with credit card offers. That has changed with new consumer finance protection laws, and now it can be difficult to get a card for them. One solution is to apply for your kids' cards from your own credit card company or a local credit union. Most institutions will set a spending limit per month, which can be helpful as your kids navigate the responsibilities of their first credit line. Reading the credit card statement together is a great parent-child exercise that will help your child understand the date when the bill must be paid, what the penalties can be for late payment, and what the interest rate is on any unpaid balance.

Providing some type of credit card for your teenager can also provide valuable peace of mind for you because as they gain independence, you will know they can access needed funds in an emergency.

ROOTS AND WINGS

As your kids grow up, turn 18, go to college, or otherwise make their ways out into the world, you're sure to wonder how your financial relationship with them should evolve. When do you teach them about taxes? How long should you provide financial support? How often should you help them out of money jams, when the rent is late or the car breaks down?

These are all important conversations, and there's not one correct answer for everyone. However, there are a few money basics they need to be familiar with, starting with those outlined in the initial chapters of this book.

If your children go to college, that period between ages 18 and 21 provides a chunk of time for ongoing growth in a fairly protected environment. During those years (college or not), they will encounter increasingly more complex financial situations, and your insight and guidance will be helpful. You can sit them down and show them TurboTax; review their pay stubs, highlighting how much gets withheld and why; and talk about the nuts and bolts of dealing with the IRS. You might consider bringing them in to meet your financial advisor as they become more mature.

Taxes aside, as your children become increasingly financially savvy and independent, they will naturally begin to develop their own priorities and values. They will grow their own financial wings. Some of that will reflect or mirror the financial values you've worked so hard to instill in them over their first 20 years. Starting from the $1 per week allowance and "Are we rich?" conversations, you've perhaps tried to convey the importance of saving for the future or giving to charity, or to instill in them values of exploration, curiosity, and compassion through travel. You've tried to lead by example and hope that they'll absorb your habits in a positive way. Now, though, as they evolve into their own people, how they spend their money could be different from how you've spent yours.

Remember, your kids' financial values don't have to be the same as yours. Do they have the financial knowledge to get started and live independently? Have you helped them acquire foundational skills they can build on? Do they know how to live within their means, the importance of saving ("pay yourself first!"), and how and why to set aside an emergency fund? Then you've succeeded. Teaching them a framework for how money works is *much* more important than making sure they spend their money in the same way you spend yours.

Still, the money conversation isn't one that is ever really finished. The wonderful thing about starting these talks early and weaving them through your lives is that, as they progress, the foundation of transparency and candor you have established will continue to serve all of you.

I can't say enough about the value of that openness here. Even though they'd done such a great job cultivating a money-confident home, I still didn't think to ask my parents for help at that terrible moment when I was laid off from my first job at 27 and didn't have any emergency savings. We hadn't established a relationship where that felt remotely possible—and they didn't offer. Many years later, my father told me he thought about offering help but believed I would figure it out. Honestly, I wish he would have said something! For all our comfort talking about money in general, I didn't have the tools to say, "I need help," and I really could have used someone with the financial acumen to tell me not to cash out my 401(k). I hope that by following the path I've laid out in this chapter, your kids will be better equipped than I was, both to make their own decisions and to ask for support when they need it.

In that way, as with every other area we've discussed thus far, it comes down to being willing to have conversations. Don't worry about perfection or awkwardness. People often think of the question of money and your children as black and white—either you're supporting them or you're not—but there's a lot more grey there. You might offer to pay specific bills while your daughter is in graduate school or to pay for music lessons for your grandchildren. You might explore setting up a 529 account to support college savings for their kids. The only way you'll know what might be helpful and where the boundaries are is to talk.

Be clear at the outset about what you will and won't do, what you can and can't afford. Then stick to it. Of course, situations can change, and agreements can be revisited. But everyone will be better served by clear conversations. You'll know what feels good and what makes sense for your family and the relationship you've built.

WHAT MONEY MESSAGES ARE YOU SENDING?

I sent my kids off to college while I was writing this book. Writing about money messages gave me a chance to consider what money messages I might have instilled in them, and it wasn't always what I had intended.

Over the years, my daughter and I have had some tearful, fraught discussions about money—how she wants to spend it and how I think she should. (I challenge you to find a mother-daughter duo that haven't been through at least one of these!)

My goal was to teach her, to teach both of my kids, to think carefully about their spending and be accountable. I do think I managed that, but it wasn't always perfect. There were times I focused so much on accountability that I may have forgotten to emphasize joy. I forgot that if she had thought a purchase through and felt it was worth the price, it wasn't my business to question it.

I'm sharing this because here I am, an expert on money and money conversations, and I can still look back and see some problematic money messages I may have passed on. I encourage you to create space for reflection as you raise your kids. In the last few chapters, you worked on figuring out the money messages you carry from your family. We defined mindsets of abundance and scarcity. Now it's your turn to look at what you might be passing on. Reflect on those money messages and consider doing more than just echoing what you were taught. Better to be purposeful about it than to look back later with regret.

CHAPTER ELEVEN

STAYING WHOLE WHEN YOU SPLIT UP

A few years ago, after two decades of marriage and several children, my friend Ayana's wife announced she wanted a divorce. Ayana is well-educated and had had a good job when she got married, but she had long stayed home to care for the kids. Post-divorce, her life changed dramatically. The couple sold their home because they needed cash to equalize their assets and pay divorce expenses. And though Ayana had been out of the workforce for nearly two decades, she needed to return to work so she could support herself and her children. How was she going to make this happen?

Another scenario: Carol had been married for 30 years when she decided the marriage wasn't working. She was the primary breadwinner, and that pressure was one of the reasons she asked for a divorce. But post-divorce, she found herself with a large house to manage on her own.

(Her husband's contribution had been home maintenance.) Suddenly, she needed a gardener and a plumber and to be prepared financially and practically in case a toilet leaked or the basement flooded. Her income was limited, but she did have equity in her house. She could start to map out her financial needs but suspected she was overlooking something.

Ayana had no idea what was going on in her own home; she was blindsided by her partner's request to split up and didn't have a clear idea of her financial situation. Carol was more informed, but she still had to play catch up when her situation changed. I've said it before, and I'll say it again: even if you're *not* getting a divorce, it's always important to know what's happening with your household finances. Money conversations and transparency, both in the easy times and during the rough patches, are central to keeping a marriage healthy. But if you haven't been keeping up, once divorce enters the picture, you may need to get educated quickly.

If you're contemplating a divorce, you're probably feeling stressed, heartbroken, and overwhelmed. But even in that context, you need to be prepared for money conversations with your soon-to-be ex-spouse and with other people involved in the divorce process. Strong emotions make talking about money especially difficult, so it's all the more important that you find a way to do it.

This chapter covers both areas: how to prepare for a difficult process and how to talk about divorce finance with your spouse, your team, and your friends—even when it's painful.

PART I: PREPARING THE GROUND

I wish I could tell all my readers who might be contemplating a divorce to put this book down and call me. But of course, that might not be viable for any number of reasons. If this is the only chapter of this book you have time to read right now, that's fine. I'm going to take you through the process step by step, and you can read other chapters to fill in the gaps as needed.

Step 1: Face the financial facts. Divorces rarely happen on a whim. As you consider whether this is the right path for you, don't forget about the money. Many people have no idea divorce is going to cost so much—in terms of money, bandwidth, and time. Because they don't really understand that aspect, they don't fully consider what it will mean financially for their families, especially if one parent has stopped working and will need to return to the workforce.

For that reason, I often suggest that people research the finances of divorce before deciding on a course of action. Doing so might make you decide to hit pause. Perhaps you will change jobs or retrain before you go ahead. Perhaps you'll decide to separate first. Perhaps you'll find another creative solution. (Also, after weighing your options, it's possible you might change your mind. I've seen it happen more than once.)

Step 2: Consider the timing. Be strategic about when to divorce. Of course, if you're in danger, you need to get out as quickly as possible. And if you're in a situation where you are hemorrhaging money because of the financial arrangements you have with your spouse, you need to act quickly. But if you do have time to build a runway, a transition period will ensure you have time to plan, so you can emerge from your divorce psychologically healthy and financially sound. For example, after asking an attorney to walk her through the potential impact of divorce on her children and the cost to her, my client Selena decided to wait until her children leave for college to seek a divorce. (This is fairly common. The kids leaving home creates a concrete landmark for unhappy spouses to tell themselves, "Just hold on until …")

Waiting has given Selena time to train for and get established in a new career. While placing herself in a stronger financial position may disadvantage her in child and spousal support negotiations, that is no reason to forgo becoming more self-reliant, which is always positive regardless of the unique marital circumstances. And it will be worth it if she decides to proceed with the divorce to know she is in a better place financially, professionally, and personally and more prepared to start a new life.

Step 3: Be discreet. As you've learned by now, communication is one of our most important relational and financial tools. However, in divorce, unfettered communication may not be the best tactic. Where one side might want to talk about how to create a happier life—either together or apart—the other might dig in and make things difficult. Some spouses may also act unethically—secretly transferring assets or making other mischief. So, in this context there are plenty of reasons to be mindful about who you talk to and how.

You will want to be able to access your financial papers without raising suspicion. When I'm speaking with women in the process of divorce, they often say, "He doesn't want to show me the financial paperwork." At some point, legally, your partner has to share it with you. It's yours, too, especially in a state like California, which considers items like these "community property." But it can still be difficult to get the information you need.

Worse, if you have a joint account, there are underhanded things that a partner might do out of spite, once they know your intentions. It's not uncommon for a spouse to take everything out of the joint account, leaving the other person without money for groceries, or to run up an enormous credit card bill just to make the other person's life difficult. Those actions aren't going to serve them well in the long run, but hurt and angry people can do a lot of damage.

Plus, divorce happens in the context of a community; most married people share friends. Remember that once you start going public, word will get around that "Jack and Jill are having problems." Being gossiped about feels terrible, especially during a period that can be painful in so many other ways. Divorce is stressful enough without people you care about (and who care about you, despite their gossiping!) speculating about what is happening.

Step 4: Consider your financial status and needs. As you begin to prepare the ground, you'll need to get your personal financial house in order as a single person and/or single-parent-to-be. The first step is determining what you own and what you owe. Typically, you and your spouse will have big-ticket items to divvy up, like your house, bank and investment accounts, and car(s). Then there are personal retirement accounts, pensions, inheritances, and belongings, which can range from pots and pans to jewelry and artwork. Next, calculate your debts. The easiest way to figure that out is to get a copy of your credit report, which is easy and free. (See Chapter 1 for more details.) Any debt you have will be listed there.

If you're worried your spouse might run up a bill on your joint credit cards to cause trouble, you might be thinking that you should cancel those cards and close or leave a joint account. But you'll want to consider the timing on this carefully and to make sure you have your own credit card and any credit card history you need beforehand. Also, depending on the law in your state, you could run into legal trouble for taking this unilateral action, even before either party has filed for divorce—so seek the advice of a family law attorney before you cancel any credit cards.

This is also a good time to think about a post-divorce budget. Figure out how much you spend in a given month or year by taking a look at your credit card and bank statements, as well as your monthly utility bills. Keep in mind that how much it costs to live your life might be a very different number once you are divorced. It's usually less expensive to live together than it is to have two separate households. In your newly single life, you might need to buy long-term care insurance or hire gardeners, babysitters, carpenters, or house cleaners to do the work your spouse did.

Spend some time looking at the activities that fill your life: the local softball league, drinks out with friends, going to the theater, family trips to see your in-laws. As a couple, maybe you go out to dinner every weekend. How's that going to change after a divorce? Once you've left the partnership, will this activity be something that's important for you? If so, include that in your "after-divorce" budget. If you have a second home, will you sell it or continue to spend summers there? If your kids go to private school, can you both swing that tuition in your new two-household context? Understand the magnitude of compromises you might have to make and start thinking about where you might be willing to make them. Your totals may not change at all—you might just have different expenses—but be aware of what they are.

Step 5: Consider your *professional* status and needs. The next part of building your runway is professional. Executing that will take preparation if you need to return to work to support yourself and your family. If you've been out of the workforce for some time, give some thought to what you will need to get back in. Will you need skills training to update your resume? Will you need access to childcare?

Ask yourself what you're best at. Who needs those skills? Who's willing to pay for them? Once you know what you want to draw income from, brush up on your strengths, address your weaknesses, and foster new skills. As always, I'm a big believer in mapping things out on paper. As we have earlier in this book, sketch out a vision and checklist for the next few years of your professional life. You'll probably need to update your LinkedIn profile and résumé and assess your tech skills. Perhaps you haven't made a PowerPoint deck in ages. Maybe it's time to learn to use Slack, Asana, or Monday.com. You may even decide you want to update your clothing style as you venture back into the work world. Whatever you need to feel more confident!

If you've been in the workforce all along but need a better paying job to meet the increased expenses of independence, you might also consider hiring a career coach. There are coaches who specialize in helping divorced women or women in transition. A call with a friend you trust for feedback and advice and a thoughtful and frank self-assessment can serve the same purpose. Take time to revisit your annual earnings. Are you getting paid what you are worth? Is it time to ask for a raise? Does a better earning opportunity exist elsewhere?

Step 6: Start working on your single-person credit score. Gaining control of your personal finances includes establishing or re-establishing credit in your own name. That can be tricky to do once you are divorced, especially if you don't immediately have income coming in. Start working on this as soon as possible to give yourself ample time to establish credit and a credit score.

The simplest way to do so is to apply for and use your own credit card. Prioritize this especially if you've only (recently or ever) had joint credit cards. Typically, the credit score is associated with the primary name on a given card. If you plan to buy a new home and are in a weaker financial situation post-divorce, qualifying for a new mortgage may be hard. A bank will consider other factors like child and spousal support, but having a healthy credit score will help. This might also be a good time to open your own savings and checking accounts, especially if you're worried your spouse might drain your joint account.

Remember my friend who insisted on buying a house in cash after her divorce? A choice like that can seem sensible because you have your home and the safety of full ownership, which *feels* safe. But that's not necessarily always the case, because buying and maintaining a home can tie up a lot of your liquidity—finance-speak for "cash on hand." It can limit your options and mean you have less flexibility. If you're facing a situation where you can't get a mortgage or even a home equity line of credit because of your income limitations, take a look at what kind of home you can afford and consider downsizing or renting. If you *do* plan to sell a home you've owned for a long time, consult a tax professional about the impact of capital gains tax before you go ahead.

One more thing to note: as you go through this process, you're especially vulnerable to making less-than-stellar financial decisions regarding your home, especially if it's the one you've lived in with your family during happier times. I get it. It's the house you raised your children in, the site of so many memories. But all that emotion can get in the way for women who are determined to stay in that house—whether "for the kids" or for themselves. They can end up owning a place they can't sustain.

Step 7: Choose the divorce that fits your marriage. You're getting closer to telling the people in your life, including your partner, what you've been thinking about. But before you make the leap, you may still want to learn more about your options and reflect on yourself, your marriage dynamic, and what makes the most sense for you.

You can start by buying a good book on divorce—whether that's *Divorce for Dummies*, a Nolo Press guide, or a reference like *Divorce in California*, which I often recommend to clients. You may also want to do a little library or internet research on divorce in your state since laws can vary; free classes offered in your area can also help with the particulars. If you're not a big reader, you might try a podcast or divorce coach (yes, there is such a thing) to help you orient yourself and navigate the beginning of the process. Divorce coaches who are local may also recommend additional resources and attorneys and mediators in your area.

Once you've done some research, you'll be more prepared to decide on the path through divorce that fits you and your marriage. This is the first of many conversations you'll have throughout this process, so talk it through with yourself before you discuss it with someone else. Would mediation be appropriate, could you both share one attorney, or do you need to prepare for a highly adversarial process? If you are lucky enough to have a track record of goodwill and communication, especially about money, mediation could be a good fit. Or you may be the kind of person who is able and willing to do all or most of the work on your own. In that case, it will cost you the time and emotional labor to educate yourself about the process and the legal ramifications of representing yourself.

PART II: MAKE IT REAL

Step 1: Start gathering financial information. Divorce is all about making an equitable distribution of marital assets and debts, which is why it helps to do a deep dive on your finances before you declare your intentions. If you are working with a financial advisor, she will ask you for specific documents in order to get an idea of your situation. If you are not working with an advisor, you can do this for yourself.

I talked earlier about what you'll need to review. Now gather copies of titles or deeds on any real estate, plus recent monthly or quarterly statements from your bank accounts, investments or brokerage accounts, and stock plans. Then comes liability: mortgage documents, bills from any car loans, student loans, or outstanding credit card debt. Use pay stubs to do the math on your income. Double check information from compensation plans, Social Security, pensions, and annuities. Make sure you have recent tax returns. And collect materials from your various insurance policies (homeowner, auto, earthquake, disability, life insurance, etc.) and estate documents (wills, trusts, powers of attorney, and advanced health directives), as well. This will all help you be in better shape going into the divorce process.

With luck your spouse will be doing this too, and you can share information. But if you're not working together well, don't despair. If you don't know where to find all these documents, my advice has long been to watch the mail, so you can figure out where your accounts are and how much is in each of them. But today most people do everything online or via an app. In that case, you can still look for bills there if you have a shared account.

Or ask some subtle questions. If you don't know where you bank—I'm always surprised at how many people are in this situation, but with the rise of credit cards and the fall of cash, it's increasingly common—you might say, "Honey, I need to get some cash, which ATM should I go to?" Or if you know your spouse works with a financial advisor or accountant but don't remember their names, you might try, "One of my friends asked me to recommend an accountant, could you give me their number so I can share it with her?" or "My mother asked me who our financial advisor is. Should I recommend ours? What's her contact information?" Over time, you can get a lot of information this way.

Once you know where you're going, you can make use of that information to get what you need. I know it sounds old-fashioned, but I advise going to your local bank branch in person and asking to speak to one of the bank managers. You might say something like, "I need to take some cash out, and while I'm at it, would you mind printing out my latest statement so I can take a look?" or "I'm doing some budgeting and would love to have a better understanding of my account. Can I get a hard copy of my latest statement? My printer at home isn't working." You may not be able to do this at the cashier's window, but someone there will be able to help you. This shouldn't raise flags. It's information you have the right to know! If you don't need the subterfuge, explain that you are divorcing and gathering documentation.

For investment and other asset information, call your accountant or advisor and ask for them to email you a PDF of your latest tax returns or quarterly report. If you're married and filing jointly, you should be signing tax returns together, so getting a copy should be a straightforward request. But if you've never interacted with the office before and they seem puzzled, you can say, "I wanted to look something up" or "I was trying to remember a detail."

Step 2: Have some initial discussions and choose an advocate. An increasing number of people are choosing to represent themselves in family court. But if you decide to work with a lawyer or mediator, ask people you trust for recommendations first, and make sure you do some preliminary research online (most have sites that describe their practice).

Once you've identified two or three professionals who might guide you through the process, schedule a preliminary conversation with each of them to learn more. Some advocates and mediators will offer a short no-cost consultation; others will charge you for the time you spend together. Plan to take notes. If you believe having a friend there for support would be helpful, ask whether you can bring someone with you. (Many attorneys prefer to meet only with the potential client, both for confidentiality reasons and to better establish a relationship.) If you have chosen mediation, involve your spouse in these steps.

Expect to leave the meeting with an overall understanding of the process you're signing up for, including complexity, consequences, and potential cost. Even if you're paying for the consultation, this is money well spent—but it won't be cheap, so you'll want to use your time well. Make sure you walk away with enough information to decide whether this person is the best to represent you and help you complete your divorce as efficiently as possible. Be prepared with a list of key questions and for a candid discussion. I've put together a list to get you started:

- Who is your ideal client?
- Do you work with more men or women? Have you worked with women like me?
- Will I work exclusively with you, or do you have associates and a team that will also work on my case?
- Can you take me through the steps of the divorce process? What will it look like for me?

- Do you ask for any money up front, and if so, how much and for how long? Will you refund the balance if I don't use the entire amount?
- How do you work to be cost-effective for your clients?
- Do I need a forensic accountant, child custody specialist, or other professional on my team? Do you work with anyone you would recommend?
- Do you have any suggestions for preparing myself or my children for this process?
- What are the next steps I need to take to get started?

Your preliminary consultation will also help you think through what the path ahead could look like. The attorney or mediator may discuss your state laws for dividing up assets. If you are the primary breadwinner, you'll learn more about your obligations. You'll probably also answer questions to help your advocate fill in details and understand your specific needs. If you are in an abusive situation and need protection, let the professional know; if you are considering selling real estate, ask about the ramifications.

If you feel comfortable with your first choice, schedule a follow-up meeting before you finish up. If not, set up a consultation with your second choice.

Step 3: Assemble the rest of your team. So much about divorce can be painful and unpleasant, but you don't have to do it by yourself. Many useful resources are available to you, including specialists with deep expertise. Along with your lawyer or mediator, forensic accountant, or custody specialist, your team might also include a trust and estate attorney, a realtor, a financial advisor, and a therapist, especially if you're having a difficult time emotionally. You'll want to be able to be vulnerable with them, so be sure to confirm that each of them is bound by confidentiality rules before you start talking about something sensitive.

Begin adding members to your team early, so they'll be ready when they are needed. Your attorney or mediator may have recommendations for you, and each new member of your team will also have ideas. As you ask around, your network will take shape.

Step 4: Update your will, trust, and legacy plans. Divorce marks the beginning of a new world for you, which means putting some thought into establishing how that world will look and work for you legally. If you were partners, and now you're not, what are the consequences for you and your heirs if something should happen to you?

According to Gallup, only 46% of Americans have a will, a figure that's been pretty consistent since 1990. If you have a will, you'll need to update it (and, if applicable, your trust) to reflect your new reality. That should happen as soon as the divorce is final. Working with an attorney on this is a good idea for most women, especially those with significant wealth or complex finances. Even if that's not you, you still need a will. You can get started using internet resources, then bring your draft to a notary near you. The process is fairly straightforward and quick.

Since you'll be finalizing your new will shortly after your divorce, now is also an opportune time to ask big questions and discuss death, inheritance, and family care with loved ones you trust. If your spouse dies while you're married and has assets such as life insurance or retirement funds, then you typically are the beneficiary of those assets and vice versa. But once you're divorced, all that changes. Now what?

If you die, your assets may go to your children. How do you want that money to be managed if they're still young? Do you want some of it to go to Aunt Beth so that she can help take care of the kids? Whom do you want to be the executor of your estate if you don't have older children or siblings to take on the task? You may decide at this juncture to work with an estate attorney to set up a revocable trust with a family member or friend as the trustee; we'll talk more about that in the next chapters. Alternatively, many people without children choose a professional fiduciary to do this work. (Note that that role is separate and different from a fiduciary advisor who manages your investment portfolio. In this case, a fiduciary is a licensed and regulated professional who oversees financial accounts and sometimes medical care or housing for clients, in various capacities both before and after their deaths.)

No matter whom you choose, you will want to have thorough conversations with each of these parties about your needs and expectations and how they'll change with your divorce. Flip to Chapter 13 for more on how to approach these sensitive but essential discussions.

Step 5: Consider spousal and/or child support. Spousal and child support are central topics, and often points of contention, in many divorces. Unfortunately, it's hard to predict how they will affect your divorce in particular because these calculations differ by state. You can expect that courts will generally take into account how long you've been married to figure out spousal support and child visitation arrangements, but your team will help you understand the nuances of your particular situation. As you talk it through with them, keep a notebook and jot down new words or policies you learn about.

Note that recent changes in federal tax laws have transformed alimony and child support systems in one important way. Before 2018, if you were getting a divorce and receiving alimony and child support, the money counted as earned income. That meant you could use some of it to fund your IRA—and your ex could qualify for a tax deduction. Now, alimony is no longer considered income, prompting a domino effect: no tax deduction for the person paying alimony means it more negatively impacts the payer's balance sheet, which makes payers less inclined to pony up, which has a direct negative impact on receivers and their children, which puts extra strain on the co-parenting relationship. This also means recipients can't use the money to fund their own IRAs, which has significant negative long-term implications for their retirement. (And since women are more commonly the recipients of child and spousal support, this policy impacts us disproportionately.)

There might not be anything you can do about this policy, but you can anticipate the issues it might cause. If you will receive alimony, ask your team for advice on planning for retirement in this new paradigm. If possible, talk to your soon-to-be ex as well, explaining the situation. It's reasonable to expect some tension here, so make sure to come at this conversation from an informational angle: you are simply providing information your spouse may not have and hoping they will adjust their behavior accordingly. Otherwise, clear communication, honesty, and empathy will help you both find a solution that works for all parties. One mediator I know recommends that, in moments of communication difficulty, you keep in mind that you're going to be coming together on behalf of your children and grandchildren for the rest of your life—so it's in both of your best interests to find your way through conflict to compromise. You might need to remind your spouse of that as well.

If you will be the alimony payer, that's a big change for you, too, one you should be thinking about before you initiate divorce proceedings. How many years will you have to pay, and how will that change your financial trajectory and future? Are there ways to distribute your assets to lessen the impact of spousal support on your long-term financial health? It's important to balance your spouse and children's real and important needs with your own; you deserve not to be taken advantage of financially. A therapist or trusted friend can help you think this through, and your financial advisor can help with financial modeling and planning.

Step 6: Look for a financial advisor who works with "women in transition." An advisor with this specialization has experience working with women dealing with death or divorce, retirement, or a financial windfall. She can help you understand your current financial picture, how it could change with your divorce—both best-case scenarios and less ideal outcomes—and how to plan for that change.

You want someone who's not trying to sell you anything, who will instead help you consider your options during and after your divorce and figure out which financial documents you'll need access to along the way. (Note that some advisors can't or won't work with a person until after they have received their settlement, since it can be difficult to predict a person's full financial landscape beforehand.) Consider asking these or similar questions before you move forward:

- How do you usually help someone who is going through a divorce?
- How many clients have you helped navigate this process and its aftermath?
- What would you charge me for your services?
- Do you have any special credentials that give you insight into divorce?
- Are you a fiduciary?
- Can you help me now, or do I need to wait until I have my settlement in hand?

You might find working with a Certified Divorce Financial Advisor, or CDFA, to be helpful as well. These professionals tend to work on a fee-only basis and can help you plan for and organize your newly single finances, mapping out how you can be whole and self-sufficient in your new life.

Step 7: Establish an emotional support system. I have focused here on the financial aspects of divorce, but making time and space for the emotional process is equally essential. Divorce can be a solitary, overwhelming experience. Some friends may be "couple-friends" and may not know how to continue socializing with just you. Some friends will disapprove of the decision to divorce. Some will be loyal to your ex.

As you go through the steps in this chapter, make sure you have a support system in place: supporting your emotional needs is an essential part of your journey to financial wellness. Make space not just for divorce logistics planning but also for letting yourself be sad and angry or joyful and excited. Walk your dog. Throw pots. Swim in a pool, lake, or the ocean.

Reach out to two or three trusted friends and ask directly for support during this time. Divorce-support may be too much to expect from only one person, but having a few confidants to lean on could be just right. Prioritize people you know to be nonjudgmental, good listeners. Not everyone will be able to do this, even if they have the best intentions. Keep in mind that it may take a couple of tries to find someone who has both the empathy and capacity to support you. But keep at it, and you are sure to find the friends you need.

Step 8: Come back to communication. Many studies cite misaligned money beliefs as a top cause of marital strife. When both people work to be financially savvy and talk to each other about money, that relieves a lot of stress. Learning how to communicate early in the marriage about finances leads to better alignment; in an ideal world, you would have prioritized making those conversations happen long before divorce entered the picture.

If you've not yet started the process but are reading this chapter because you're unhappy, it's worth considering how you might get more aligned to possibly stay together, even as you consider your options. Have you been keeping up with Money Dates? Have you taken the time recently to talk through your financial priorities as a couple? If you're on the same page about staying home on Friday night because you're saving to buy a house, or if you both understand that you're camping instead of staying at a pricey hotel because you'd rather pay down debt, then there's room to get excited about making these choices, *choosing* the quiet night in and the campground, rather than fighting about it.

And if you know divorce is where you're headed, you can still improve your money communication at this late stage, in part by seeking solutions that fit you and your soon-to-be ex. Doing so will still help you get through the divorce process or mediation with less pain. It may even help you find a way to be friends later.

Every divorce is different; there are so many ways to go through this process and emerge intact financially and emotionally. So, I can't tell you there's any one "best practice" for communicating through the worst of it. But I can say that creative solutions and compromises are essential to the best outcomes. Remember Carol, who divorced after 30 years of marriage? Despite the love between her and her (now-ex) husband, they had a hard time in mediation. They owned not one but two valuable homes—but not much liquidity or savings. It was hard to figure out how to equalize since the houses were worth different values, and they had little cash. The conversations around this sometimes became too painful, requiring them to stop and regroup.

In the end, they decided to write each other into their new wills, making each other 20% beneficiaries. In this way, they could pay each other later and still move forward. It was a lovely way to acknowledge that they had built and stewarded these assets together and to stay connected to some extent. Finding that solution took a lot of conversation, a lot of trust, and ultimately, a lot of love. From where you're sitting, it may feel hard to believe that love is still there—but, through communication, you just might find it.

CHAPTER TWELVE

YOUR MONEY, AGING, AND LEGACY TALKS

My father's best friend—we called him Uncle Bill—was in his sixties when his wife died. Not long after, he sold his home and moved into a retirement community. A former college swimmer, he was still in good health and could enjoy daily time in the community pool, making new friends and creating a rich solo life for himself.

My father, by contrast, always felt strongly that moving into a "home" was the worst thing that could happen to him. He reluctantly visited a handful of nice assisted-care facilities, but in his mind, all eldercare was a death sentence. After my mother died, he lived on his own for many years but became increasingly lonely and depressed, which led to further decline. When he reached a point where it was unsafe for him to drive, and he wasn't taking proper care of himself, we finally convinced him to move into a retirement community, but by then it was too late for him to create a new routine or build new relationships. He lived there for two years before he passed away, yet he was never able to get into a mindset that would allow him to adapt.

My father was 87 when he died. I believe that if he had made the move earlier—say, when he was 80—he would have made new friends and enjoyed his remaining years in far greater health and happiness. In my view, Uncle Bill's move extended his life by many years because he built a new community for himself. Looking back, I wish I had talked to my father earlier about the options he had beyond a "traditional" nursing home or an assisted living facility and how those options could improve his quality of life. But he was so adamant for so long that I was afraid of even bringing the topic up. Honestly, I felt I was a bad daughter because I couldn't do more for him and I lived so far away.

While we've touched on the basics of talking about money with your parents, we need to go deeper. Even in families that have great relationships, money conversations push emotional buttons—*especially* with aging parents. (If there's one thing we fear more than talking about money, it may be talking about death.)

If you're in the "sandwich" generation, old enough to have kids but still with healthy parents, you're in a dual transition period. After years of your parents being in charge of everything, you and they may begin to realize that they need help—perhaps just as you begin to more seriously plan for your own later years. If you're lucky, you can have calm, rational conversations about aging, talking through your parents' more immediate needs, and figuring out your own desires and plans for retirement and old age along the way. You'll identify potential issues, engage professionals to support you, and take steps toward the best solutions for everyone.

If you've just laughed at this idea because it sounds ludicrous and impossible, stay with me. It can be a minefield, but don't worry. I'll walk you through it.

TOUGH TALKS, LEAVENED WITH TENDERNESS

Just as I am an advocate for building a financial conversation habit with your spouse or partner through Money Dates, I also recommend making time to discuss your plans for your life as you age. In my industry, "legacy planning" includes not just making plans for after your death but also all those discussions that come along with it, including your hopes for the last stages of life. So, I call the conversations in which we explore these thorny issues Legacy Talks. We'll spend the last two chapters of this book on Legacy Talks and all of the challenging themes they can address. How do you want to age? How do you want to die? And how do you want to go through all of it together? Because if we're lucky, it's not something we'll do alone—but we'll need the right financial infrastructure in place to make our vision a reality.

Legacy Talks can help you have conversations with your parents about their plan to age in place. They can also create opportunities for discussions with your partner about retirement and funeral planning, and heart-to-hearts with your children about your fear of dementia. You can have these conversations on a weekly or monthly basis, in whatever format you like. And you can use them both for talking about aging, as we will in this chapter, and for talking about death, as we'll discuss in the next.

These chapters are meant to be read together, guiding you as you build what is likely to be a new or under-exercised muscle. If you start by talking with your parents about aging, as discussed in this chapter, that will help you consider potentially scary questions about your own later years—how you want to plan that stage of yourself for yourself or with your partner or children. And those conversations about aging may lead naturally into discussions about death, which can be employed in conversations with your partner, parents, or anyone else important in your life. (Thus, though our discussion about Legacy Talks may not always explicitly say so, you can and should apply the questions and prompts you find useful for other contexts or relationships.)

Some Legacy Talk best practices, which are similar to those for Money Dates, include:

1. Eat first. Everyone is always in a better mood if they aren't hungry.
2. Keep it to an hour. You can always schedule additional meetings to learn more or go longer once you are comfortable. If you have to go over, make sure to stop at 90 minutes. These conversations are usually a lot to take in, and keeping everything within a manageable time frame will help.
3. Bring a notebook and create a list of questions in advance that you'd like to cover.
4. Consider creating an agenda and sharing both the agenda and your list of questions in advance of your meeting.
5. Reward yourself at the end of the hour. Take a walk, have some ice cream, treat yourself to a latte.
6. Space out meetings so everyone has time to think of questions they forgot to ask or bring extra information they want to share.

BRINGING UP AGING WITH YOUR PARENTS

Legacy Talks with your parents will involve multiple conversations. Key topics to make sure you cover include financial planning, what to do if parents do not have enough resources as they age, the possibility of downsizing, whether they should invest in long-term care insurance, and what to do if one or both of them begins to suffer from cognitive decline.

Before you dive in, put yourself in your parents' shoes. What was their upbringing? What is their comfort level with this topic? Approach your conversations with compassion and patience. Remember that you are asking them to talk with you not just about money but also the inevitability of decline. They may be facing the real prospect of losing independence, which for many people is difficult and frightening.

If your dad was always "the guy" you called to fix everything, if he is used to being in a helping or leader role, just be aware that this could be an especially tough conversation for him. You might have a dad who is the best husband, father, and employee but didn't know much about finance or wasn't a great saver. Maybe your mom is amazing too, but she was never involved in the money conversations. She might feel shame about not being able to provide enough for herself or her family.

Instead of creating an agenda right away, aim to meet them where they are. One exercise that might be helpful: before you begin the conversation, get clear about *why* you want to talk and how it might benefit them. A mindset of "I want to have this conversation because I think it might create peace of mind for them," is preferable to "Will there be any inheritance?" Think of this conversation as a mission of love and an opportunity to talk about something that affects everyone's well-being.

Then, take some time to consider how you'll bring it up so that your parents are receptive to your questions rather than upset by your concern. Here are some possible ways in:

- Share with your parents that you're starting to put your own finances in order and ask them how they have thought about their plans.
- Frame it as asking for advice and guidance for yourself: you're trying to plan for your later years and don't know quite how to go about it. Ask what your mother did or what her parents did. Tap into their wisdom and parental inclination to share advice and experience.

- Use the example of a friend or relative whose sudden change in health required the whole family to make myriad adjustments. "I've been remembering when Aunt Alice got sick and our cousins had to scramble. I want to make sure we are able to work together as a family through sudden changes like that."
- Be your authentic self, and don't be afraid to be vulnerable. They are your parents after all! You could try, "I get worried that with all the different things I'm juggling—family, work, kids—if you need me, I might not be able to get to you as quickly as I need to. I want to be there, and I want to be able to help. Can we do some planning together?"
- Use whatever is prompting you to have this conversation as a starting point. Maybe they've been talking about a special trip, planning a big wedding for one of your siblings, or selling their home. Then you'd say, "Mom, Dad, I've heard you talking about selling your house. I've been thinking about my finances and doing some planning too, and I wonder if we could talk about finances. I could use your advice."

When you've chosen which approach feels right for you, find a few minutes of quiet time when everyone is calm, and it's just you with one or both of your parents. Maybe you're having breakfast together, are on a walk around the neighborhood, or are driving somewhere. Don't be surprised if they are not receptive. On the other hand, they might surprise you and be happy you're asking. Maybe they didn't know how to bring it up, either.

Take cues from how your initial question or comment is received. If you have never had this kind of conversation with your parents and they seem open to it, your next step could be to say, "How would you feel about setting up some time to talk about your retirement?"

If they're resistant—"Everything's fine! What are you talking about?"—then consider addressing their issues later and instead pivot to your concerns. In that case, go with, "Mom, I've been thinking about my finances and the future, and I'd love to talk about it with you." Or, "You mentioned your back has been giving you trouble lately, and it made me wonder if you and Dad have long-term care insurance." Or maybe, "I know you're helping Maria plan her wedding. Could we talk about family finances more generally?"

GETTING ON THE SAME PAGE

Your first Legacy Talk with your parents should focus on sharing goals, hopes, values, and prior preparation. Start by discussing what they want as they grow older—the possibilities for retirement and the next 5 or 10 or 20 years. What are the values they want to focus on during this time? Do they see themselves traveling, spending more time with grandchildren or on hobbies? Asking these questions helps open the door for more finance-focused inquiry, even if they're outside the specific focus of aging and money. I've come up with a few possible ice breakers you might start with:

- Have you thought about how you're going to spend your time in your retirement? What will your week or month look like once you retire?
- What aspect of retirement are you most excited about?
- What relationship would you like to have with your grandchildren, and how can we facilitate that?

Then move into the essential details:

- Do you have enough to retire comfortably? How do you define "comfortable"?

- Have you calculated your expenses—weekly, monthly, or annually?
- How are you managing healthcare? Do you know what Medicare will cover?
- Do you have any pension, personal retirement assets, or Social Security benefits that will provide an income once you are no longer working?
- Have you considered moving or downsizing?
- Have you talked with a financial advisor?

You might quickly discover that their financial house is in order; they just haven't been sharing that information with you. Ask them if now might be a good time to start sharing. If they respond positively, consider requesting a checklist of all the "nuts and bolts" of their finances. Keep the list somewhere accessible but secure, and update it at least once a year. Don't be offended if they are not ready to discuss numbers, or any of this, with you; they also may not be ready to bring you into conversation with their advisor. Knowing that they have a plan is still likely to provide some peace of mind.

(You can also use this format to talk with a partner or your own children about your future. In that case, that "nuts and bolts" list is still important but so is making sure you've filled in whoever you're talking to about what you've already done, what you've yet to take care of, and where you hope to go from here. That shared foundation will be essential to all the conversations that come next.)

EMOTIONS AND LOGISTICS

The difficult conversations we need to have about aging can generally be divided into three categories: broaching the subject, emotional/vulnerable content, and logistics. I recommend designating time explicitly for each category, and in that order: first you break the ice on a particular topic (health directives or planning for cognitive decline, for example); next you talk about all the feelings that topic brings up; and finally you discuss decisions you need to make or action steps you need to take.

As you transition from one area to the next, I'd urge you to remember that you're likely to be moving in and out of both practical and emotional issues. That can be tricky, but just keeping that in mind will help you be more patient with each other. If you anticipate you might have a tough time, your agenda and question list can serve as a map to guide you.

Acknowledging your discomfort can also be a powerful motivator and connector. Rather than feeling embarrassed or ashamed that you're not handling this better, it's okay to say, "I'm uncomfortable talking about this, but I think it's important that we do." You might even *start* your talk by sharing some of your own fears and desires. Your vulnerability will pave the way for others to share as well.

Eventually, though, you will want to transition to logistics and an action plan. Without the nitty-gritty details and decisions, it's hard to make your ideas a reality. Let's say your parents want to age in place. Do they need to add ramps, grab bars, a stair climber, a ground-floor bedroom? Would they do better in a smaller home? As usual, I recommend you map it out together. What will it cost to execute this vision? How does this fit into their budget? Do some research to find relevant numbers to plug in.

IF THEY AREN'T PREPARED

It's entirely possible that you may find in these conversations that your parents haven't done much thinking and preparing (and saving) for retirement or end of life. Hopefully, this won't be the first inkling you have that they haven't made plans—although if it is, I promise you aren't alone.

If it turns out that they may need your help in the future, then your next step is figuring out the scope of that support. You'll want to get a handle on their financial assets and resources and a sense of how they want to live the rest of their lives.

You can have that first conversation, figuring out whether they need your help. And you can follow that with the third conversation, figuring out what the help you're going to give them looks like. But let's linger for a moment on the discussion in between, the second conversation, which requires so much vulnerability. That's the one where you say, "I know I'm your child, and maybe this feels awkward. But Mom, Dad, I want to help." It may be hard for them to hear, but if you come to the discussion with a spirit of open-heartedness and cooperation—"I'm a little concerned, and want the best for you, how can we do that together?"—then that will help remind them that you have their backs.

Once you move to putting together an action plan, remember that you don't need to get your parents through this by yourself. How much money they have, how much you have, and how much they need are all findable numbers, and there are plenty of financial professionals who can help you find them—whether their stockbroker, your CPA, or an advisor or planner you engage together. If you're figuring it out on your own, try to aim for an amount that supports them without derailing your own personal financial journey, so you can give happily.

Then, you can choose from any number of different ways to help. Sometimes, adult children decide to pay their parents' property taxes directly or underwrite the cost of their health insurance. Sometimes they become co-signers on their parents' bank accounts and set up auto-pay for bills. Sometimes it makes sense to help sell a large home that no longer makes sense financially and find a more affordable living situation that meets their parents' needs at this stage of life.

Don't make the mistake of thinking that because you're approaching this with compassion, you shouldn't formalize it, just as you would any other financial transaction. Writing things down does not injure your parents' dignity or mean you love them any less. You may not need a formal legal agreement, but everyone will benefit from a written record that all parties understand. Remember that a central part of this puzzle is understanding what your financial obligation to your parents will be. Financial independence means being able to take care of yourself and the people you love, but it doesn't mean the latter *at the expense of* the former.

WHY YOUR PARENTS MIGHT NOT HAVE ENOUGH

If your parents are in their seventies or eighties today, then that means they were born shortly after World War II. They probably started working in the mid-1960s, with their peak earning years in the mid-1980s. They may have worked for the same company their entire career. That was common: companies expected employees to stay at the company long term and offered incentives such as defined benefit plans or private pensions as motivation to stay.

For much of the late twentieth century, people would buy a house and pay off their mortgage over 25 or 30 years, with the aim of retiring with a house they owned. Once they retired, their pensions and Social Security benefits generally allowed them to live out their retirement years comfortably. But the burden of providing for retirees became an increasing liability and less desirable for companies. In 1978, Congress passed the Revenue Act of 1978, in which Section 401(k) cleared the way for the establishment of defined contribution plans and sweeping change. According to the Employee Benefit Research Institute, by 2011 under 10% of employees had employer-sponsored pension plans.

Instead, in 2014, the US Bureau of Labor Statistics reported that three-quarters of employees had access to defined contribution plans (such as a 401(k)) and were expected to contribute to and manage the lion's share of their own retirement funds. That meant employees were responsible for their retirement savings and investments in a way they never had been before. With very little financial training or access to solid advice, they often did not save enough or invest in a way that ensured they would have enough for their retirement years.

And on top of all of that, life expectancy increased dramatically during this time. With the onus on them to manage their own retirement savings and make them last much longer, it's no surprise that many people of this generation are unprepared financially for their retirement—and that their children are having to step in. It's not their fault, but now it *is* our problem.

Most current workers expect to retire when they are 65, but the median retirement age is 62. That means people often retire before they plan to. Some encounter health problems or disability; some are healthy but retire to take care of an ailing spouse. Some see their companies close or fall victim to downsizing. If your parents fall into the demographic of people who are on the verge of outliving their assets, you probably feel obliged to help them. That's an admirable impulse, and I encourage you to follow it. But as with all things in life, there's only so much you can control.

We can control how much we spend and how much we save. We can control where we decide to invest our money. We have some control over how much we can earn and for how long we can earn it. But then we are faced with all the things we *can't* control: market returns and tax policies; political, cultural, or economic events that affect the market; natural disasters that affect our jobs, housing, or communities; personal crises that balloon our expenses, such as sudden illnesses or deaths; and decisions our parents made before we all started communicating.

All of this is to say that as you and your parents survey the terrain you're going to travel together, remember all this and act accordingly. Save where you can save—not just the minimum of what you think your entire family is going to need. Make sure you have a plan in case the market goes against you just when your parents are going to retire. Aim to keep one or two years of cash (or equivalents) on hand in bond investments, money market, or savings accounts as the time grows closer. And stay on top of your contingency plans. If you have a mental map of what you might do even in the worst of times, it will help you let go of what you can't control. Then your parents' retirement becomes not just about survival but about peace of mind.

IT MIGHT NOT BE TOO LATE

Even if your conversations with your parents reveal that their financial situation is precarious, it may not be too late to do something about it. If your parents are still a handful of years away from retirement, they may be able to improve their prospects. While they still have income, they can prioritize paying off outstanding high-interest rate loans like credit card debt. They can make catch-up contributions to their 401(k) and IRA accounts—especially since once they've passed 50, they can put more money into both those accounts.

If they're in good health, they might consider buying long-term care insurance (see later in this chapter). Once they are 65, they qualify for Medicare, which will impact their healthcare costs. They can review their Social Security payout so that they know how much they are likely to receive and at what age, because it makes a difference at what age they opt to begin drawing Social Security. If they can afford to wait to draw on their Social Security, that may make the most sense for them.

Another factor to consider is where they'll live. How would they feel about selling their home and moving to a town where the cost of living is lower, especially a town near friends or relatives? What about a supportive community that offers progressive care as they get older? Have they considered refinancing their current mortgage? (While some people continually refinance their mortgages when mortgage rates are low, many people hold onto high-rate mortgages simply because they don't know that refinancing is an option.) Be sure to consult a tax professional if you're thinking about selling a home, since that can have significant tax consequences.

One last possibility: many retirees begin an encore career once they retire from their main jobs. Others opt for something with less pressure that keeps them engaged in the community. It might not pay big bucks, but it can cover basics like groceries and gas.

If your parents plan to retire in the next several years, or are worried about getting pushed out early, help them think about what they might do now to prepare by saving more, adding new skills, or scaling back their expenses to a level that they will be able to maintain long term. They will have many more options while they are working than they will after they retire; some doors close after retirement because applicants without a job often won't qualify. For example, it can be difficult to refinance a mortgage if you are not employed. That's why it's important to act as early as you can.

Even if you started these conversations focused on helping your parents, you may find that your Legacy Talks inspire you to think about your own plans. Perhaps it's time to initiate these conversations for yourself. You still have a chance to give yourself a running start on things like investments, health insurance, life insurance, long-term care insurance, and overall expenses. If understanding your parents' financial situation prods you to get started or get serious, turn back to our chapter on investment, and get going.

CONSIDERING LONG-TERM CARE INSURANCE

If you or your parents are just at the beginning of planning for older age, don't underestimate the importance of long-term care insurance, which makes a great Legacy Talk topic. At first blush, long-term care insurance may seem like a luxury. But even with an able-bodied spouse, it's a lot to ask someone to care for all your daily needs, and if you are single or without children to help you when you can no longer manage for yourself, it can be especially beneficial. According to LongTermCare.gov, someone turning 65 today has almost a 70% chance of needing long-term care services and support in their remaining years. Yes, that means one third of today's 65-year-olds may never need long-term care support. But 20% will need it for longer than five years. (Plus, statistically women tend to need care for 1.5 years longer than men. That's a big difference when these services can cost thousands of dollars a month.)

The psychology behind long-term care insurance is a little complicated. You might buy it, never need it, and end up feeling like you wasted that money. But it's important to acknowledge a "sunk cost" dynamic that encourages people who have the insurance to use it. It's easier for people to use services they feel they've already paid for. If you need in-home care, you're much more likely to get it for yourself if you have a pot of long-term care insurance money waiting to be spent. That decision could positively, and profoundly, impact your daily life. In contrast, sometimes even if people have money saved for a specific use, they're hesitant to spend it. And there may be some psychological barriers to accessing it even if they want to—for example, if that money is invested in a stock portfolio which they've earmarked for their children.

If you're still on the fence, ask yourself if you or your parents can "self-insure" or save enough for the eventuality of long-term care. If yes, then long-term care insurance is probably unnecessary because you can pay out of pocket for the services you need. Even beyond that, if you save up the money and you need to spend it, will you be willing to do that?

If you decide you want to go forward with long-term care insurance, AARP recommends shopping for your long-term care policy between ages 60 and 65, when you are young and healthy enough to buy it affordably—and even then, it is likely to be expensive. Typically, the longer you wait, the more expensive it becomes. Sometimes, adult children contribute to the cost, since they recognize that having the funds from a long-term care policy will help them care for their parents in the best way possible. If you're the adult child talking to your parents, you may want to bring this up as a topic of discussion along with everything else; if you're considering this for yourself and have adult children, it's worth engaging them in conversations on the topic.

FACING UP TO DEMENTIA

As the population lives longer, cognitive impairment and dementia are on the rise. For many people, the prospect of losing their memory, or having to watch a partner do so, is even more frightening than death itself. Since financial advisors navigate dementia in our work quite frequently, we see firsthand how important it is to talk about rather than avoid it. We know that having a plan soothes an anxious mind and can be comforting during times of crisis. If your partner, parent, or another loved one does decline, you will regret not having had the chance to speak to them when you could. It's worth pushing through any discomfort to engage—if only so you know you have connected and heard each other on the topic.

One way to approach the subject is to bring it up in a Legacy Talk, after you've built valuable momentum, confidence, and trust through less sensitive conversations. You might also consider using media, such as the affecting film *Still Alice* or the charming Netflix series *A Man on the Inside* as jumping-off points for discussion. However you do it, make space at the beginning to talk about your feelings, especially if dementia runs in your family or you have personal experience caring for a loved one in cognitive decline. That will make it easier to engage with the practical aspects of this topic.

Whether the focus is on yourself, your partner, or your parents, having this conversation early makes it much easier to make contingency plans for how you might delegate responsibilities and decision-making, helping you put safeguards in place in a way that makes everyone comfortable. As you plan, you'll want to put legal scaffolding and financial infrastructure in place and create a list of resources.

Because financial advisors have such an up-close view of cognitive changes, it's a good idea to speak with yours if you have one. Some advisors have more experience with this issue than others, so ask about her experience. To start the conversation, you might ask, "How do you approach dementia in your clients? What are signs you'd be looking for down the road, and what actions would you take?" You'll also want to talk with her or with an estate or elder attorney about how to establish durable power of attorney in case you or a loved one develop dementia. (That is a legal document that allows you to give someone else the power to make medical decisions on your behalf if you cannot make them for yourself.) At my firm, once we've talked about this protocol with our clients, with their permission, we often begin including a designated younger family member in emails and in meetings so the family is kept in the loop regarding their loved one's portfolio. This helps keep things on track if they become difficult for the client.

If, instead, this conversation is happening in the context of active decline, you'll want to get clear quickly on where your loved one has access to finances so you can monitor accounts. It's not unusual for someone who is forgetful or confused to fail to pay the mortgage; to make unusual or outlandish purchases; to make donations to a favorite organization many times over, repeating whenever they forget and remember again; or to fall prey to online scams. This is where having power of attorney in hand becomes paramount.

YOUR BEST IS WORTH SOMETHING

Even decades later, I still find the contrast between the stories of my father and Uncle Bill striking. They were great friends in part because they were so alike. They both had two kids; they both lived in similar situations and were of similar economic means; and, eventually, they both outlived their wives. Yet one spent his last years with a great sense of community, while the other struggled, feeling much more alone.

I wish I had been better prepared for these tough conversations with my father. Even when I did try to engage him on the subject, we made little headway, and I quickly withdrew. The truth is, I was scared! Writing this chapter has allowed me to reflect on how much courage it takes to have these fraught conversations with people we love.

As in many chapters in this book, I see lessons I had to figure out on my own that I want to help you avoid. In this case, what I learned is this: don't wait. If you're caring for an elder in decline, act sooner and with more purpose than I did.

I hope this chapter will help you feel empowered to make a move, to think, "I don't want that for my parents or myself; I'm going to find the courage to have this conversation today instead of tomorrow." Don't worry about perfection. Engage with your parents if they're still around. Talk to your partner and your children about your vision for retirement and beyond, while you have time to fine-tune your plans, long before you need any of the infrastructure you're so carefully building.

And, as we approach the end of the book, there's one more truth worth acknowledging: not all conversations work out the way you hope they will. You might prepare well, have the best intentions, and still not get the outcome you desire. Even though my initial attempts to talk with my father about assisted living did not convince him, I know that I did the best I could with the skills I had at the time—and, all these years later, I'm still glad I tried. Even if your own conversations don't get the outcome you hoped for, knowing you did your best will bring you a modicum of peace.

CHAPTER THIRTEEN
DEALING WITH DEATH

My friend Prithi had been married for 20 years when, suddenly and unexpectedly, her husband had a massive heart attack at work one morning and died. He was in his late fifties and had been in apparently very good health. It was quite a shock.

It was also financially devastating. Theirs was a two-career, two-income household, and they had recently canceled their life insurance policy as part of broader cost-cutting measures. Not only had Prithi lost her life partner, but she was suddenly in a precarious position in terms of supporting herself and her children.

Three years later, I'm happy to report that Prithi now lives in a new home that she owns. She has made real strides in expanding her savings and building up a nest egg. She has increased her retirement savings and created a budget for joy. And she has a roadmap to retirement, even after facing such an enormous setback. All that is possible because she made a series of smart choices, even in the face of so much sorrow—and because she sought out effective conversations with friends and, eventually, a financial advisor.

First, she considered her options. She owned a home but was worried about carrying the mortgage and expenses on her own. She thought about a roommate but decided she didn't want to take one on. Then, she wondered if she might be able to make some extra income by renting out a room via Airbnb, but the COVID-19 pandemic hit, disrupting that market. She also thought about taking on extra work as a caregiver, but ultimately that wasn't necessary.

Prithi's friends created a GoFundMe after her husband's death, and that financial cushion helped support her through the first six months. During this time, she asked me to help her think through the many financial decisions she needed to think about, since this is my area of expertise. We worked together using an online "intelligent investor" platform to invest that money so it could continue to support her down the road.

Next, we talked through a series of questions about her expenses and generated a working budget. Once she understood how much she needed every month, we could identify where she could trim her spending to make up for her husband's absent second income. We also adjusted her retirement savings plan accordingly. We had to be creative about where she might find some income, even outside of how she'd made money in the past. Finding an extra few hundred dollars a month by reducing several smaller expenses like online subscriptions and by budgeting more carefully with groceries made a real difference over the course of a year. That helped her reduce stress during such a heartbreaking time.

Preparing for death goes against our human instincts. We would much rather pretend we'll live forever. But death is a fact of life. In the last chapter, we talked about planning for aging, especially with our parents and grandparents, who usually die before us. According to Kiplinger's personal finance news, more than one million women are widowed every year, with half of those over 65 outliving their husbands by 15 years or more. And eventually, you too will die, although of course I hope it will be painless and after a long, happy life.

These difficult truths dictate that, as daunting as the prospect might be, preparing for your own death and that of your loved ones is the smart and compassionate thing to do. One route through this difficult material is via a series of key conversations.

LEGACY TALKS—PART 2

My parents talked about death all the time. At nearly every holiday gathering, usually after dessert, they would say something like, "It's wonderful to be here with all of you, and we are so grateful for everything we have, but who knows what next year will bring? We might be dead. You never know."

These speeches were so regular that they became a running joke between my sister and me. We would be sitting at the Thanksgiving table finishing our turkey and discussing how grateful we were to be together, and my parents would decide it was the perfect time to bring up their demise. It was so predictable, and so absurd, that we could do nothing but roll our eyes. (In retrospect, this was likely a product of their childhoods. My parents grew up during World War II. My father's father died when he was in his twenties, and my mother's parents both passed away when she was very young.)

Now, though, I consider that habit from a different perspective. Yes, these conversations felt morbid, but the philosophy behind them also meant that my parents lived their lives more fully, acknowledging that someday they wouldn't be around. My father may not have planned out his life after my mother passed away, but both he and my mother *were* thoughtful and organized about their deaths.

Talking about aging with various family members in your previous Legacy Talks will help you build confidence talking about your and their deaths. If you have trouble getting your partner, parents, or children on board, or if you struggle yourself, that's okay; it may take many tries. In fact, the serial aspect of these conversations is key given how much potentially fraught material there is to cover. Don't go in thinking this is something you need to accomplish all at once. You might designate a few Legacy Talks to consider what you want in your will, others for funeral and burial preferences, a couple more for creating a Health Care Directive.

My guidance from Chapter 12 applies. Beyond your parents, remember that you can use this technique to engage anyone in your life about your, or their, death. Choose a cadence that works for you: don't meet when you're likely to be hungry or tired; set aside a specific amount of time, and don't go over that limit; and reward yourself afterward. Time checks are one way to ensure you're respectful of your conversation partner's capacity for painful content. One version: "Gosh, this is a lot, and we've been talking for an hour. How do you feel? Do you want to keep going, or should we set a follow-up time and finish up for today?"

SWEAT THE DETAILS

Since my parents lost their own parents when they were very young, they planned ahead for their deaths. They had insurance and a current will, and as they got older, they engaged an attorney who specialized in working with older people to make sure everything was in order. When we were young adults, they asked my sister and me to list and agree on the things we each wanted from their belongings. They paid for all their funeral expenses in advance; my dad outlined what he wanted in his obituary. He even made a cassette tape—it was 1983!—which he left in his safety deposit box that instructed us on what to do with the cars ("Sell one and keep the other, and here's the name of the mechanic.") and the washer/dryer ("They're pretty new and should last 15 more years.") and included thoughtful, poignant messages for each of us.

So, when my father eventually died in 2011, both my sister and I expected that everything would be in order. We sold the house and divided up various belongings and didn't have a single negative discussion about who got what, although we did trade a few items back and forth. But there were two questions that hadn't been answered: Did Dad want organ music at his funeral? We decided no. And did he really want his obituary published in the newspaper, which was going to cost $400?

Full disclosure: We had a fight about it. While we did sort it out (we ran the obituary and shared the cost), this story shows that even with the best-laid plans, during times of high emotion, people will argue about anything that is not nailed down.

My sister and I are close, and we worked out a solution. But the fact that our family had talked about everything, written it down, and agreed on it in advance helped us through the aftermath of our parents' deaths and laid the foundation for a stronger relationship once our parents were gone. My parents gave us a model for talking about death with others, a lesson I want you to keep in mind during these conversations: unlike in most circumstances, when it comes to Legacy Talks, you do want to sweat the details.

STARTING THE CONVERSATION

Even if you did well talking about aging with your parents, discussing death with them, your spouses, partners, and kids won't be easy. We're so unused to talking about death that even starting the conversation can feel uncomfortable. Luckily, many of the approaches you used for talking about aging can also be helpful here, especially if you can use those conversations as a springboard. If you're looking for a way in, here are some possible starting points. (These tips are aimed toward a partner but can be adjusted for talking with your parents or others.)

- Try something broad and not too personal. For example, you could use media you read or saw recently as a jumping-off point: "I just read an interesting article about life insurance I'd like to share with you. I'd love to hear your perspective."
- Keep your comments focused. Let's say you don't know what kind of life insurance you have or how much you have. You might start out gently, saying, "I was talking to some of my friends about their financial plans, and it occurred to me that I don't really know what kind of life insurance coverage *we* have. Could we take some time to talk about that and our other plans?"
- Make it about them, not you. Say, "I'd love to talk about life insurance. If something happens to me, I want to make sure that you're covered."
- Shift the focus to your kids. You might try, "I want to make a plan so you and the kids can stay in this house if something happens to me," or "I want to make sure the kids will be fine if something happens to one of us."

If you receive a negative response, it might help to remind yourself and your conversation partner that this is, ultimately, about exploration, conversation, and connection; it's a chance to know and understand each other better. Legacy is about money, yes, but it's also about the relationships we leave behind. I often think about how my dad liked to build and fix things, or how my father-in-law built a 50-year business that supported his family. All of us have stories from our lives and lessons we have learned that our loved ones will want to know. These conversations are a way for you and your partner or family to get to know each other on an even deeper level and talk about what's important to you. They're acts of love.

GETTING YOUR DOCUMENTS IN ORDER

Documents are a good place to start in your Legacy Talks about death because they're concrete and practical, less connected to all the fears that make conversations about death so difficult. You're likely to have discussed, and perhaps even gathered, these documents during your conversations about aging. But you'll want to make extra sure you have them easily accessible in the case of your loved one's death—or your own. Not all of these may apply in your specific situation, but here's a starter list of materials to gather:

1. Trust and estate documents
   - Will
   - Revocable/irrevocable trust
   - "Incapacity documents" such as a general/durable health power of attorney and an Advanced Health Care Directive (also known as living will)
2. Financial documents
   - Name and phone number of your financial advisor
   - Banking and brokerage statements
   - Safety deposit box location and key (This might also be a good time to add another name and signature to the safety deposit box account, to ensure someone will always be able to access it.)
   - Recent income tax forms, W-2 forms, or other record of earnings
   - Notes payable and receivable
   - Banking passwords and PINs
   - Credit card statements
   - Student loan documents

3. Miscellaneous but still important
   - Code, password, or key to a safe or secure area where documents are kept (if different than safety deposit box)
   - Insurance statements
   - Car registrations
   - Business agreements and contracts
   - Real estate deeds
   - Social Security numbers
   - Military discharge papers/VA claim number (if applicable)
   - Marriage and birth certificates
   - Passports and drivers' licenses

WILL VERSUS TRUST

If you or your parents don't yet have a will or trust, that should sit at the top of your high-priority topic list for Legacy Talks about death. Our legal and financial system for handling someone's affairs after they pass away can be complex, making planning ahead especially important. To start, every adult with assets needs a will to ensure those assets are distributed according to their desires. In many states, if the estate in question is relatively simple—a house and partner but no kids, maybe, and fairly straightforward accounts—that might be enough. (You will need to select an executor, someone to manage the will after you die.)

You don't have to have a trust. Not everyone needs a trust, and the process of setting up a trust can be expensive so it's not a decision to be taken lightly. But once you start accruing assets that you'd like to pass on to the next generation, and your financial life has greater complexity, it's probably time to consider setting one up. One reason for this is to avoid "probate," the court-supervised process of settling an estate and dealing with the deceased individual's will, assets, and property. Probate is rarely quick, easy, or pleasant, although some states' processes move faster than others. Working through probate can require plenty of paperwork, court appearances, and the fees you must pay to make both things happen. The longer it takes, the more fees you may incur, including executor, attorney, and administrative expenses.

More drawbacks: first, probate is a public process—and you may not want the fact that you just inherited an apartment building or that your uncle had a second family enshrined in the court record, which anyone can access and read. Plus, unless you are the joint owner or beneficiary, you may not have access to funds within bank or brokerage accounts going through the probate process until it is finished. That can take months, sometimes years.

As a solution, many people establish revocable trusts for their assets well before their deaths. When you establish a revocable trust, you make the trust the owner of your assets. Then, when you die, a named trustee distributes those assets according to your wishes and pays taxes on your behalf. Establishing a revocable trust keeps the distribution of assets private and allows you to avoid probate. Specifics around revocable trusts can be complicated, and they differ by state. A financial advisor or trust and estate lawyer can tell you if a trust is worth the time and money and, if so, what type of trust might work for you or your parents' situation. What's crucial to understand for now is that creating a trust will help clarify your desires, maintain your privacy, and make distributing assets after a death much easier. (If you want to avoid creating a trust, you may have the option, instead, to add a "transfer on death" [TOD] designation to your accounts, in which you can designate a beneficiary to directly receive your assets when you die. But this is not possible in every state and may not solve all of your problems. Make sure you ask a financial expert what works best for your situation.)

Some people work with "elder attorneys" to set up a trust. The National Elder Law Foundation certifies lawyers as Certified Elder Law Attorneys (CELA), recognizing their specialized knowledge and commitment to this practice area. An elder attorney can also help you with qualifying for

Medicare, navigating personal and legal issues in your family after a spouse's death, obtaining Social Security and other spousal survivor benefits, and lots more. Make sure you ask about their fee structure and experience advising on your particular issues before you begin working together.

FINDING YOUR REPRESENTATIVES

A trust and estate attorney friend of mine recommends that her clients focus on "three picks" when planning for their futures and building infrastructure for their eventual deaths: a healthcare proxy (as we discussed in Chapter 12), a guardian for any minor children, and a representative to manage the will or any revocable trust.

Representing a loved one after they die can be both emotionally and logistically complex. If you're approaching a family member or friend about being your executor or trustee, I recommend you first write a memo to/for this person, explaining what the role typically entails, why you want them to fulfill this role, and any essential logistics or details. (Maybe your parents would become co-guardians of your kids, but they don't have a lot of money. In that case, it's important to let them know that you've, for example, set aside some funds that can be used on your kids' behalf.)

When you make your request, you might start with, "I have updated my will, and I would like to designate you as my executor (or the guardian of my kids or my trustee). Is that something you'd be willing to do for me?" Or you could say, "I need to designate a new _____, and it needs to be someone besides my ex-spouse. I'd like to ask you if you would fulfill that role." Chances are, they aren't going to know exactly what that entails, so you may need to explain. Then, you can say, "I'd like to set aside some time to fill you in on what that means to me." Sitting down and reading through the memo together can make for a deeply meaningful conversation. Then answer any questions they have and hug each other.

If you are single and have no kids or obvious person to be the trustee, you might consider appointing a professional fiduciary to handle your estate. If you're looking for a professional to fill this role, you'll want to be thorough in your approach. Here are some questions to ask:

- How long have you been doing this work?
- How big is your firm? Do you work solo or with other people?
- If I get in touch with you, how long will it take for me to hear back?
- What is your succession plan? Who will handle my account once you retire?
- Are you willing to work with other professionals, such as my estate lawyer and financial advisor?
- Could you connect me to three clients who might be willing to talk about their experience working with you?
- What are your fees?
- What is your accreditation?

In this case, too, you will likely want to write a memo, sometimes known as a "letter of wishes," expressing your values, your vision for the assets, and any details you think would be important for anyone handling the account—for example, the people who take over once the fiduciary you chose retires. You can add this to your will or ask the fiduciary you work with to keep it on file.

UNDERSTANDING LIFE INSURANCE

As you consider your mortality and the mortality of the people you love, investing in inexpensive term life insurance to protect them is a good preparatory step. Before doing so, you'll need to discuss it with your loved ones. A Legacy Talk is a great time to educate yourself and figure out your plan.

When clients ask me if or when they should get life insurance, my answer is almost always, "It depends." Whether you are the breadwinner or a stay-at-home parent, you are responsible for many tasks that keep your home running and life humming. Basically, once you start to have people in your life that depend on you financially (kids, retired parents, etc.), you should be thinking about life insurance.

While there are many types of life insurance, the two most popular kinds of life insurance are *term* life insurance and *whole* life insurance. For the purposes of this book, we'll focus on term life insurance. (For the record, whole life insurance, also known as "permanent" life insurance, builds cash value and covers you forever, if you continue to pay the policy's premiums.) Term life insurance is a fixed amount of insurance, for a fixed price, and for a fixed period.

If you work for a company, typically, your company offers some sort of term insurance. (Note that the insurance will almost certainly not be portable if you change jobs.) Many people also buy their own term insurance when their kids are young, to cover them for a period, typically 10, 15, or 20 years. During this time, you and your spouse are working, saving up, making investments—you're in "accumulation mode." While you're in that mode, it makes sense to have life insurance, to guarantee your family will be cared for in case one of you dies. (This use of life insurance is sometimes referred to as "wage replacement.") But once you've grown your assets, paid down your mortgage, and built a nice portfolio to fall back on, you might not need that safety net, and you may decide you no longer need the policy. If you're not sure how long your "term" should be—when you'd be safe not being covered by life insurance anymore—you can ask your advisor to look at your portfolio and do a capital-needs and cash-flow assessment.

If you have a full-time job, your first step should be to go to your HR person and ask, "Do I have life insurance? If so, how much do I have?" You may be covered and not know it. If you're not covered, or self-employed and without an HR rep to talk to, the next step is to find a life insurance agent yourself, perhaps starting with recommendations from friends or your financial advisor. One caveat: many people are suspicious of insurance and of insurance agents, since they work on commission. That may be true, but it doesn't mean you don't need what they're selling. There are many very good, trustworthy insurance agents who will take the time to explain every aspect of what you are buying and how much it will cost you to buy it.

Ask your agent what your "death benefit" will be. Many people save for their retirement but don't have an emergency fund for next month's expenses, since their job is paying for those. So, ask yourself: if the primary breadwinner in your family suddenly dies, how much insurance money would you need to allow you to pay for many months of "next month's expenses" *and* continue saving for retirement? Will your surviving spouse need to return to work after being a stay-at-home parent? If so, will there be enough to pay for childcare expenses? Will the proceeds be enough to pay the mortgage and support your family's current lifestyle?

If you're young and healthy, you should be able to sign up for life insurance pretty simply. (While you're at it, you might ask if you have disability insurance through your employer and consider signing up if you do not. After all, you are more likely to be disabled unexpectedly than you are to die suddenly.) If you're older, are buying a lot of coverage, or have pre-existing conditions, you will likely need a physical exam. In that case, it may be in your interest to work with an insurance broker; brokers represent several companies instead of just one and can find the one that will insure you at the best rate.

MAKING DIGITAL ARRANGEMENTS

Another Legacy Talk topic: planning for *digital* death. It used to be that all you needed to do to prepare your accounts for the inevitable was to make sure you had all your documents in a safe place. But dying has become infinitely more complicated in the internet age. Handling a loved one's digital footprint after a death can feel almost as daunting as dealing with the emotional and financial side of things. There's email; there's social media; there are accounts with recurring charges—payment apps, Netflix, Amazon, Dropbox. In the age of two-factor authentication, making sure you have access to your partner's or parents' accounts with a backup method of access—and that they'll have access to yours—is crucial, so that you can close them and stop paying monthly or annual fees.

During your Legacy Talk on digital preparedness, you'll want to strategize how you'd want news of your deaths announced (or not) on social media, build your list of accounts, and identify priorities so it's not overwhelming for one of you later on. Start by making a list of account usernames to keep somewhere safe, along with password information, and make sure your loved one knows where the list is—or better yet, use a password management app that will securely hold and manage the information. Star or otherwise indicate any accounts connected to a monthly or annual bill. When the time comes, you will want to prioritize managing, closing, or transferring them into your name first. That will prevent you from wasting money and getting a painful reminder on your credit card bill every month. (Best practice is to create a separate, password-protected document that can be accessed in the event of your death. At the very least, avoid listing your passwords and pin numbers on a piece of paper.)

Apple also now allows you to designate legacy contacts, one or more people who will be allowed to access your account after your death. The system generates a key you share with your nominated contact. After a death occurs, the contact gets a few years to view messages, photos, and files and make decisions about what happens to all of it. Google has a similar system, known as "Inactive Account Manager." You specify when Google should consider an account to be inactive. After that amount of time passes, automatic messages are sent to nominated contacts, as with Apple. Your designated contact will get access for a few months, or you can also opt to have Google delete the whole account. And Instagram, Facebook, and X all have systems for deactivating an account upon receipt of a death certificate and other data about the deceased person. You might designate these contacts together as an activity during your Legacy Talk or assign the task as homework and check in in a week to make sure you both followed through.

NAVIGATING WIDOWHOOD

Losing your life partner, feeling your grief, and navigating all the tasks required in handling post-death logistics is a lot for anyone to handle. If you haven't previously steered the family finances, you may need help sorting everything out. During this vulnerable time, you may receive calls from individuals offering their services as financial advisors or in other professional capacities. While you are recovering and identifying your next steps, tell any callers that you've already engaged an advisor, so that no one pressures you. Take their name and say you'll call if you need to or ask them to send you information. It's okay to wear your skeptical hat. Verify any advice and consider getting a second opinion.

This also may mean protecting yourself from well-meaning friends. I've met recently widowed people who had a family friend step in and offer to assist, but sometimes the friend didn't know much more than the bereaved person. Of course, any true friend has only the best intentions and wants to be as supportive as possible. But they can do more harm than good if they don't have the proper training.

I'm not saying you should never accept help, only that you should be cautious. Don't be afraid to ask about the credentials of anyone offering assistance. Use your judgment about when to go with a professional versus someone who is street-savvy. Just because this isn't someone's day job doesn't mean they can't be helpful to you. But even in your time of need, you still owe it to yourself (and the people who rely on you) to make sure that the financial advice you're getting is valid and in your best interest. If you're unsure how to ask, I've come up with some possible scripts:

- "I appreciate you stepping forward to help me. Can you tell me about your experience doing this kind of work?"
- "I'm just curious, have you dealt with this before?"
- "Have you worked with a lot of widows? How has that become an area of expertise for you?"

As you navigate this new role, you will need to prioritize certain actions, like closing and converting accounts. If you did the work beforehand to prepare, as discussed at the start of the chapter, you made this task much less complicated for yourself—but that doesn't mean it's less painful. It can be hard to keep it together when your grief is so recent. So don't; make sure you leave some space for yourself to fall apart.

Maybe you're fine with the task itself but would appreciate general support or cheerleading. Ask a friend to come over and sit with you while you sort through the paperwork, make calls, and close accounts.

Unfortunately, there's no shortcut or alternative to this slog. And some things do need to be addressed quickly. Make a list—banks; charities;

deeds to property; life, health, car, property, casualty insurances—and go through it methodically, at a manageable pace. Set a timer and go through one chunk at a time; play music and take a break when the timer chimes. See if there is anything you can do in a friendly place like a neighborhood café. After a big chunk of work, do something kind for yourself.

LEAN ON OLD SKILLS AND GOOD FRIENDS

In the first chapters of this book, we've talked about the power of budgeting and the complexities of good and bad debt and other financial fundamentals. If you're taking the financial reins of your family for the first time, I encourage you to go back and review those sections. Your relationship with these topics may change now that you're sailing solo. If you are new to managing your household finances, take time to assess your financial needs and plans to understand where you are now. Once you've done your assessment, are there any changes you need or want to consider?

Do you want to or will you need to set up new budget? If so, return to our sections on that topic. You'll also find plenty of helpful advice on this topic on Reddit, newspapers or magazines, and finance podcasts.

Or do you have an inheritance, money from a life insurance payout, or another asset and are unsure what to do with it? Sometimes people will use a windfall to pay off a mortgage. The intentions make sense, but I recommend hitting the pause button for one to three months while you are adjusting to your new situation and figuring out your options. If you don't already have a financial professional who can help you with these decisions, consider talking to a loved one or a friend before you pay off your house or make other big moves. If you're unsure how to start the conversation, try,

"Could we talk confidentially about something? I have so many questions and am learning about my options."

You might consider adding team members to fill in the gaps, such as a professional organizer, accountant, or financial planner. Even if your friends don't have the knowledge to help you, they might still serve as a sounding board and be able to help you find helpful resources. You know who and what is right for you. It's natural to feel alone in this circumstance, so think of your support team—loved ones, advisors, friends—as your safety net.

NEXT STEPS

Really, what I'm trying to do in this chapter is urge you into conversations and actions that will help you avoid regret. The more I realize my time on earth is finite, the more proactive I am in making sure I live each day as I want to, connecting with the people I care about. It makes me prioritize what is important to me.

If you'd like more opportunities to explore this topic, talk to some of the friends you trust to be your support network when the time comes, to share information and resources now. Friends who have seen you through multiple life stages and important events are especially helpful, and they know that you will return the favor.

I have a circle of friends I've been close with for decades. In the beginning of our friendship, a lot of our conversations were about our work, partners, and children. Now, we're empty nesters and talk a lot about what that means and how we want to spend our time over the next 10–20 years; sometimes we talk about our hopes and fears for the next part of our lives. These conversations have brought us closer, increased the trust between us, and allowed us to feel okay asking for support. I imagine that as we age that will extend to include themes covered in this chapter more often.

If you have similar people around you, nurture that resource. If you feel the need, you could acknowledge, "This may seem weird but ..." and then ask your opening question ("Have you made a will yet?" "How did you go about creating your Health Care Directive?" or "Have you and your partner done any funeral planning?").

If you'd rather read than talk, I recommend two books on this topic: *The Good Will*, by Elizabeth Arnold, and *The Art of Dying Well*, by Katy Butler. Arnold's book helped me consider both the financial and emotional side of death. Her book helped me see that wills aren't just legal documents but can be heartfelt emotional tools and should be treated as such. Failure to put together a good will can really be destructive, but when you do it well, it can be a powerful way to pass on your legacy.

Butler offers poignant advice as well as practical tools for planning around death, as well as a philosophical and spiritual approach to the topic. Actuarial models indicate that one in every couple is likely to live well into their eighties or nineties. So, what do we do with that time after a partner has passed? How do we maximize quality of life? Butler has lots to say here.

These and so many other good books are just a library visit or Bookshop.org spree away. Spend some time in a nice reading chair, with pen and paper (or whatever you use to jot down ideas and notes) and feel good about the work you're doing laying the groundwork for important conversations and movement toward the end-of-life you want.

Catching up with Prithi, I can report that it's not been an easy road for her, but I'm so proud of how she's come through this difficult time. After the shock of the first year, she eventually found new sources of happiness and fulfillment. She adjusted her savings and budget and was able to continue the work she loves while remaining on a path to retirement around age 65. She is careful to maintain her budget for joy, which for her means traveling. She keeps costs down by doing a house exchange or staying in inexpensive accommodations.

In my mind, she serves as proof that having your spouse unexpectedly die is terrible, but it's not insurmountable. With prior planning, careful thought, grit, time, community support—and, most importantly, conversation—there's life on the other side. But really, isn't that true for so many of life's troubles?

EPILOGUE

WELCOME TO THE CLUB

I've always loved to read. Books transport us: They take us places we might never go and teach us things we might never expect; they comfort and educate us. And you don't have to be a financial geek to see that books are full of financial lessons waiting to be learned.

Take *The Great Gatsby*. For me, that book is about what money symbolizes and how it can transform us or serve as a vehicle for vengeance or love. Jay Gatsby is in love with Daisy. He lost her and has spent much of his life trying to win her back. He thinks his money is the key that will unlock her love: if he has the right shirt or the right house for the right party, she will come back to him. But that's not the case. Ultimately, they are from different worlds and classes. She can't cross that barrier to reach him—and she doesn't want to. Why is that? In part because of their different relationships to money. His use of money feels performative and insecure, whereas she is used to knowing her money will always be there. The lesson I take from that book is how important it is to find a partner whose money messages are compatible with yours—and to spend your money the way you want to, not how you think other people think you should.

Great Expectations is another one of my favorite books. To me, it's a book about the consequences of tremendous deprivation and then opportunity. The main character, Pip, believes the rich, mysterious Miss Havisham is paying for his education and opportunity to escape poverty, when in fact his benefactor is a former convict who is quietly repaying Pip because Pip helped him when he escaped from prison. Readers see the power of a good deed to change more than one life. To me, the takeaway is about the power of charity and the importance of paying it forward.

In *Vanity Fair*, Becky Sharp is perceived by her community as a conniving, heartless woman who will sell her soul for money. But I would argue that Becky has very few options. She either lives by her wits, or she will go hungry or worse. The book challenges its readers to consider how they might behave differently under similar circumstances. What steps might they take to prepare for that possibility?

And in *The Merchant of Venice*, we learn about the perils of moneylending. The story features plenty of still-familiar pitfalls, even some 400 years later. What can we learn from Shakespeare about credit cards that charge 20% interest on unpaid balances?

Why am I talking to you about all these literary classics? As you've seen here, even in great works of literature, characters face the same issues we flesh-and-blood humans do when it comes to money. Once you start finding financial lessons as you read, it's hard to stop. At this point, I can't help but see them everywhere. I ask myself, "If they had handled the money differently, how would these characters have fared? How do I avoid stumbling over the same issues they faced?"

You have come to the end of this book. I hope you feel enlightened, strong, and excited. You might think, "Okay, I read the whole thing.

I learned all this stuff. I'm ready for my next steps ... Wait. What *is* my next step?"

I want you to finish this book not just with new tools and newfound feelings of confidence when it comes to making choices around your money. I want you to feel empowered and supported. And I want to help you create a network of people around you who control their money instead of letting their money control them—people who will support and shape your relationship with money in positive ways.

That's why my last suggestion to you is to start a financial book club. This club will help you create a sustainable community where you can explore the topic of money, figure out what it means to you, unchain yourself from unhelpful money messages, and find greater control over the money in your life. Your club will be about collaboration, can-do spirit, friendship, authenticity, and purpose. Even after you finish this book, you don't need to continue this journey alone. It's more fun to do it with friends.

A NOVEL EXPERIENCE

You might think I mean you should read more how-to books on finance. While that is one option, I'm actually suggesting you form a club for reading novels—in a very particular way. After finishing up here, you might feel like you need a break. So why not start by reading fiction?

Reach out to a few friends or colleagues and invite them to join you in reading a book you love with interesting financial themes—whether it's Edith Wharton's *The House of Mirth* or more recent fare like Miranda July's exploration of money, desire, and menopause, *All Fours,* or the Pulitzer-prize winning *Trust.* For many people, reading fiction and thinking carefully, analytically, and in-depth about the role money plays in the story is more comfortable than picking up *The Wall Street Journal* every morning. You can enjoy reading books that interest you while also maintaining your newfound money management and communication skills—if, as you read, you keep an eye out for financial tethers within the plot, consider how money affects the characters, and discuss how you might behave in a similar situation. This "financial novel club" can be a source of a community and a jumping-off point, where you can continue both building muscles for talking about money and cultivating greater financial knowledge. Here are some questions you might explore with each title:

- What was the role of money in this book?
- How did money impact the lives and the decisions of the characters?
- What positive or negative things happened as a result?
- How did money affect these characters' relationships with their community?
- Did one of the characters experience a monetary gain or loss? How did that change things? How would you have handled it differently?
- What are parallels you see in your own life? How can you take what you learned and apply it for yourself?
- Is anyone in our group facing a challenge that appears in the book right now? Has anyone faced something similar in the past? What collective knowledge might we share?
- If more than one person is facing this challenge, is there an expert we could invite to teach us how to navigate it?

That last question is one advantage of a club: you can invite speakers to come talk about any topic you like. Maybe someone in the club knows a trust and estate attorney she can invite to come and speak. Perhaps someone in the group got divorced last year and can invite her lawyer in for a discussion. You have a built-in audience and an excuse to learn!

Before you know it, you will have been meeting for five years, reading novels, talking about their financial themes, and finding resources together to meet life's financial challenges—from returning to the workforce to experiencing widowhood or navigating health crises. Because a financial book club is about reading books together, yes. But it's also about building a community where you can support each other.

ABOUT MY CLUB

My conviction about the power of a book club comes from more than 20 years as a part of a 12-member club. The consistency of meeting monthly is surprisingly powerful, and over the years my fellow club members have become very close friends.

The structure is simple. We meet once a month. At the beginning of the year, we send out a spreadsheet for the year ahead, so everyone can pick a month they want to host. Whoever is hosting that month picks the book or chooses a few possibilities so we can vote. We read books of all kinds; this isn't a money-focused club. I love the breadth of what we read! Sometimes, if we're really into it, the discussion ends up taking the whole evening. If the author is local, we might invite him or her to come and do a reading. (You'd be surprised how many writers are open to this, and I bet there is a published author in your town.) Then we adjourn to dinner and enjoy the evening chatting about whatever we want. Sometimes that's more about the book, and sometimes not.

Molly, a good friend of mine, has been a member of a similar club for several years—one that *is* focused on money in the way I'm recommending for you. All the members came to the club with very different but fairly rudimentary financial knowledge. Through their reading, they've been able to talk about strategies, educate themselves, and compare experiences.

Some members have been able to pay off debt in part thanks to what they learned in the club, and all of them report having a better understanding of family finances. They feel more in control of their savings, know how to create an emergency savings plan, and have been encouraged to think more about their retirement. They've transformed their financial lives as a result of coming together consistently in this way. That's what this book club can be for you too.

WHO, WHAT, WHEN?

If you're going to be learning and growing together, it's also helpful if you and the other club members share some things in common. You might be new parents and all want to know more about how to raise financially savvy kids, so you create a list of books that will illuminate money-and-parenting-related topics. Maybe you're all young, single women and want to read books about people your age so you can learn together about savings, investing, and spending. Or perhaps you are employees navigating an IPO, and you will look for books set in Silicon Valley. Regardless, your commonality will provide fertile ground for you to work through these issues together. (But don't underestimate, as well, the value of a diverse set of ages, experiences, and life situations in adding to the conversations you can have together.)

You *will* want to keep the group to a manageable number. We chose to keep our club at 12 members since that's about the biggest crowd any of us can host at our houses (plus it means we each host once a year!). You should also establish some organizing principles: In person or online? Potluck or hosted? Meet indoors or talk as you hike?

Get all this down on paper and go find friends who want to take that journey with you. Then get together and decide on a roadmap. That might even include planning out dates for the first six months. Putting things on your calendar helps them feel real, and having common goals and vision will help you see things through. That will also help you keep meeting after that initial new-club excitement wears off, no matter how well-intentioned the members of the group might be. Make sure to schedule meetings often enough that there is continuity and accountability, while remaining manageable for all the members.

This can look however you want; the important thing is you settle on a realistic structure. Then comes the fun part.

AT THE FIRST MEETING

At first, some club members might feel awkward about talking about money together, especially if you don't know each other well and have never talked about it. That's natural. And that's the glory of a book club: it gives you a way in. To overcome the sense of a taboo topic, take time during your first meeting to discuss and define your club's purpose and to create a code of conduct. Here are some guidelines you might consider:

1. Follow so-called Vegas rules: what we talked about here stays here.
2. Avoid hard numbers. None of us need to disclose what's in our bank account. Talk in percentages and concepts but not about specific amounts of money. No one needs to share numbers to talk strategy. (Sound familiar? It should.)
3. Eschew "context clues." If you're talking through the process of buying a new car as a group, one member might be deciding between a Mercedes and a Jaguar, while the person next to her is thinking about Honda Civic. You don't have to signal your wealth by saying you're considering a fancy car. Keep it general!
4. Remember that there are no stupid questions. Many people are afraid to acknowledge that they know less than other people do (or than they think other people do). But if everyone comes to meetings with the idea that they're here to gain and share knowledge, that creates a more even playing field.

After you've set your ground rules, you might do a "get to know you" activity. An ice breaker serves two purposes: getting people comfortable with each other and getting them on the same page. Go around the room and answer these questions: "Why are you here? What would a successful book club look like for you? What are you willing to do to make sure it's successful?" (If you don't already know each other well, you might consider starting most of your meetings with ice breakers, until they don't feel necessary anymore.)

Don't worry if some of the club time is taken up with general chatting. By definition, when people come together, there is a social element, so make sure to leave room for that. Still, the point here is mutual learning and growth. I strongly suggest picking a book or an article to discuss, even on your first time out. That's one way people can have vulnerable conversations about money without necessarily feeling that they have to reveal a lot about themselves.

WHAT'S NEXT?

The last story I'll share with you in this book is about an acquaintance, Lorna. After enduring an unhappy marriage for many years, she finally decided recently to get a divorce. She had put the decision off for a long time, knowing that a divorce would change her life dramatically. She was sure to lose both most of her money and time with her children.

Two things changed: first, the kids went off to college. Then, Lorna came to stay for five days with her friend, Devi, to clear her head. Devi and her husband Dan are happily married, and while the three of them didn't explicitly talk about divorce during the visit, they didn't have to. Afterward, Lorna sent Devi a note, saying, "I just want you to know that spending time with you and seeing how you interact with your husband helped me remember what a healthy marriage looks like." The experience showed

Lorna that she had been waiting too long to make a change—but now she was ready. "I know I'm going to struggle financially, but my freedom is worth that," she told her friends.

That's a very vulnerable thing for a self-sufficient woman to say, even to people she trusts. But I'm happy to report that Devi and the others in Lorna's circle have responded with deep kindness and generosity. They encouraged her to begin meeting with a financial professional, to ensure she has expert support. And they have made sure she's getting more phone calls, more invitations to dinner or to visit, more spontaneous check-ins. These little moments of support—"I was thinking of you and thought I'd say hello," "Is there anything you need?"—have helped Lorna be brave in a moment of profound personal and financial uncertainty. She understands that all the money in the world won't make her marriage better. She's able to jump off the cliff because she knows her friends will be there to catch her.

I'm telling you this story because we've come to the end of our time together. You may not be navigating divorce on the cusp of retirement, as Lorna is. But even so, my hope is that, as Lorna did, you'll find living, breathing resources beyond the pages of this book: real people who can support you as you practice money communication and navigating your finances to make money work for you, helping you make progress toward whatever goals you might desire.

At the beginning of this chapter, I mentioned the panic you might feel as you flip to this last page: "Uh oh, now I have to go back to being an adult by myself. What do I do next?" But you're not by yourself. Half the advice in this book isn't about money at all; it's about making connections and having conversations. If you don't know the answer to something, I guarantee you someone else you know is in the same boat. And this is the kind of boat that's more comfortable when you have company. If you ask someone your question, and by chance it turns out they do know the answer, then great, you now have a resource!

EPILOGUE

One of your most valuable tools in your money journey is *vulnerability*, the kind Lorna has shown and her friends have responded to. Find someone else that you can talk to, a friend, and share what you're thinking about, worrying about, going through. So much growth can come from just going to a friend, or two or three, and saying, "I've gotten to a point in my life where I would like to understand my personal finances a little bit better, and I'd love to talk through some of my questions with you." How would you react if someone came to you and said that? I'm guessing it would feel pretty good.

Thus, as my parting thought, I'll issue you a challenge. Put the book down and try to connect. My generation would pick up the phone; if that's not who you are, send a text or a DM or invite a friend for a walk. However you do it, it's time: reach out and start your next conversation.

APPENDIX (CHAPTER 9)

LIFE TRANSITIONS SURVEY

Your Name _____ Date _____

Directions: In each section, select the transitions that you are currently experiencing and those you are likely to experience in the future. In addition, check transitions in the short-term and long-term columns that you either hope to experience or anticipate with concern.

APPENDIX (CHAPTER 9)

	Life Transitions	Currently experiencing	Anticipate short to mid-term	Anticipate long term
1	Change in career path			
2	New job			
3	Promotion			
4	Job loss			
5	Job restructure			
6	Education/retraining			
7	Sell or close business			
8	Transfer family business			
9	Gain a business partner			
10	Lose a business partner			
11	Downshift/simplify work life			
12	Sabbatical/leave of absence			
13	Start or purchase a business			
14	Retire			
15	Phase into retirement			
16	Other:			

Life Transitions Survey

	Financial Life Transitions	Currently experiencing	Anticipate short term	Anticipate long term
1	Purchase a home			
2	Sell a home			
3	Relocate			
4	Purchase a vacation home/timeshare			
5	Re-evaluate investment philosophy			
6	Experience investment gain			
7	Experience investment loss			
8	Debt concerns			
9	Consider investment opportunity			
10	Receive inheritance or financial windfall			
11	Sell assets			
12	Other:			

APPENDIX (CHAPTER 9)

	Family Life Transitions	Currently experiencing	Anticipate short term	Anticipate long term
1	Change in marital status (marriage)			
2	Change in marital status (divorce)			
3	Change in marital status (widowhood)			
4	Expecting or adopting a child			
5	Hire childcare			
6	Child entering adolescence			
7	Child with special needs (disabilities, medical/dental problems)			
8	Child w/pre-college expenses (private school, tutor, lessons)			
9	Child going to college			
10	Child getting married			
11	Empty nest			
12	Family special event (Bat/Bar Mitzvah, anniversary party, special trip)			
13	Helping and/or gifting grandchildren			
14	Concern about aging parent			

Life Transitions Survey

	Family Life Transitions	Currently experiencing	Anticipate short term	Anticipate long term
15	Concern about health of spouse/partner or child			
16	Family member needs caregiving			
17	Concern about personal health			
18	Provide for long-term care (parent, spouse/partner, or self)			
19	Disability/hospitalization (self or family member)			
20	Death of family member			
21	Other:			

APPENDIX (CHAPTER 9)

	Legacy Life Transitions	Currently experiencing	Anticipate short term	Anticipate long term
1	Increase charitable giving			
2	Give special financial gifts to children/ grandchildren			
3	Give parental pension (monthly stipend)			
4	Develop an estate plan			
5	Change estate plan			
6	Develop an end-of-life plan			
7	Other:			

Used with permission. Copyright Money Quotient. Founder, Carol Anderson & President, Amy Mullen. See more at https://www.moneyquotient.com/about/team/

MORE RESOURCES

General personal finance

- *On My Own Two Feet* by Manisha Thakor and Sharon Kedar

Career planning and changes

- *Working Identity* by Herminia Ibarra
- *Getting Unstuck* by Timothy Butler
- *Switchers: How Smart Professionals Change Careers* by Dawn Graham
- *Take the Leap: Change Your Career, Change Your Life* by Sara Bliss
- *What Color Is Your Parachute?* by Richard Nelson Bolles

Home ownership and real estate

- *Rich Dad Poor Dad* by Robert Kiyosaki
- *The ABCs of Real Estate Investing* by Ken McElroy

MORE RESOURCES

Abundance and scarcity

- *The 7 Habits of Highly Effective People* by Stephen Covey

Divorce

- *Divorce for Dummies* by John Ventura and Mary Reed
- *How to Do Your Own Divorce in California* by Ed Sherman

Death and dying

- *The Good Will* by Elizabeth Arnold
- *The Art of Dying Well* by Katy Butler

Further reading for your financial novel club

- *The Great Gatsby* by F. Scott Fitzgerald
- *Margo's Got Money Troubles* by Rufi Thorpe
- *Great Expectations* by Charles Dickinson
- *Vanity Fair* by William Makepeace Thackeray
- *The Merchant of Venice* by William Shakespeare
- *The Dutch House* by Ann Patchett
- *The House of Mirth* by Edith Wharton
- *All Fours* by Miranda July
- *Trust* by Hernan Diaz

Further watching

- *Mary Poppins Returns* (on balancing family finances)
- *Still Alice* (on navigating dementia)
- *A Man on the Inside* (on navigating aging, widowhood, and dementia)
- *Marriage Story* (on divorce)

ACKNOWLEDGMENTS

The longer I am on this earth, the more I appreciate that nothing truly wonderful happens in isolation.

While writing is a solitary process, no book finds its way to you without many hands nurturing, shaping, and championing it along the way. It does take a village, and I feel particularly blessed with the village that surrounds me.

The journey from idea to manuscript is not an easy one, and *It's Time to Talk* would not be what it is without the contributions of Alissa Greenberg. Thank you, Alissa, for sticking with me and helping me get this over the finish line. I feel we crossed it hand in hand.

Every gem, no matter how promising, cannot realize its full potential without a masterful cutter. Mine is Connie Hale, development editor extraordinaire. Ruthlessly strict yet endlessly encouraging, she helped make this manuscript shine. Thank you, Connie, for your confidence that this could be a book that not only would help others but would be something they would want to read.

ACKNOWLEDGMENTS

I'm also particularly grateful to fellow mom and author, Bridget Quinn. She recognized both my passion for teaching women, teens, and young adults about financial fundamentals and my conviction that financial literacy equals financial empowerment—and saw that, together, they could make a book.

Attorneys and advocates Jenny Wendell-Lentz and Katie Burke and CFP Margery Neis provided invaluable feedback on my draft chapters. Performance coach Trevor McGregor saw that I had a book in me 10 years ago and helped me appreciate that "where focus goes, energy flows." Other cheerleaders and collaborators include my literary attorney, Robert Pimm; my author friends, Phil Lerman and Dr. Cindy McGovern; my colleagues, Angela Giombetti and Steve Jans, who believed in this project from the beginning; and my colleague, Joe Bragdon, who raised his hand when I asked for help finding a publisher. Joe introduced me to Nick Magliato at Penguin Random House, who in turn introduced me to Sara Noakes at Wiley … and here we are.

Writing this book has been one of the hardest things I've done. In fact, now that it's finished, I'm amazed that books ever get written. The credit for creating the book in your hands or playing in your ears goes to the team of professionals at Wiley, including Sara and her colleagues Sherri-Anne Forde and Katherine Cording. You are my dream team and ideal readers.

Finally, I want to express my deep appreciation to my family. While my parents have passed, I know in my heart they did their best in supporting my sister and me, and I am grateful for their efforts.

To my children, Athena and Cooper, thank you for being my audience when I was practicing my presentations, providing feedback on the content, and putting up with all the money conversations we've had over the years.

And to my husband, Jason: thank you for reading, editing, and championing this project from the beginning. Your tireless support and deep belief have meant everything to me.

ABOUT THE AUTHOR

Sheila Schroeder moved to the United States from Asia at age 7, the child of a Japanese mother and a German American father. Through high school and college in Indiana, a formative time in Tokyo, and a multi-decade career on Wall Street, she developed an understanding of personal finance that has enabled an independence she deeply cherishes. Her appreciation of the freedom that comes with financial empowerment has inspired her to help other women find that same agency.

Sheila was part of a group of Wall Street pioneers who were the first women to rise through investment banking's ranks in the 1980s and 1990s, paving the way for generations of younger women to follow. A decade ago, after more than 20 years focused on the Japanese and Asian markets, she shifted her attention from institutional to individual investors, where she found her passion. She has led business development for multiple registered investment advisors, serving most recently as a consultant and Regional Head of Business Development for Wealthspire Advisors, one of the largest and fastest growing wealth advisory firms in the United States. She has spent

ABOUT THE AUTHOR

the last decade leading financial literacy workshops and speaking to audiences across demographics on the most important topic people are least comfortable discussing. An avid hiker, reader, and cook, she lives in London with her husband.

INDEX

A
AARP, 213
The ABCs of Real Estate Investing (McElroy), 69, 256
Abundance mentality, 150–151, 168, 180
Affordable Care Act (ACA), 37
Alimony, 14, 194–195
All Fours (July), 241, 256
Allowances, 93, 159–160, 163, 165, 171–176, 178
Anderson, Carol, 149
Annuities, 189
Apple, 233
Arnold, Elizabeth, 237, 256
The Art of Dying Well (Butler), 237, 256
Asana, 186
Asset allocation, 117
Asset leveraging, 65–66, 127, 137

B
Bag lady syndrome, 32
Balanced growth portfolios, 59
Bankrate Emergency Savings Survey, 19
Bengen Rule, 23–24
BIRDS (budgeting, investments, retirement, debt, and savings), 164
Bliss, Sara, 38, 255
Bolles, Richard Nelson, 255
Brainstorming, 34, 82, 140, 149
Budgets, 41–55
 allowances vs., 159–160
 automated, 46
 case study of, 219–220
 for charitable giving, 76–79
 for children, 163–164
 choices in, 49–50
 for families, 102, 168
 financial advisors for, 111
 financial information for, 190
 financial planners for, 109–110
 for freelancers, 52–53
 of friends, 104
 and frugality, 36
 for housing, 48

INDEX

Budgets (*Cont.*)
  importance of, 54
  for joy, 237
  and layoffs, 136
  in marriage, 158
  for parents, 207
  policies for, 48–49
  for political donations, 80
  post-divorce, 185–186
  rules for, 45–51
  and salary negotiations, 125
  and savings, 45, 51–52
  spending cutbacks in, 47
  strategies vs. numbers in, 94
  for student debt, 72
  visuals for, 50
Buffet, Warren, 170
Burnout, 142–143
Butler, Katy, 237, 256
Butler, Timothy, 38, 255
Buyouts, 136–137

C

CalPoly, 74
Capital gains tax, 187
Capital-needs and cash-flow
  assessments, 230
Cash flow statements, 46–47
CDs (certificates of deposit), 8, 61
Center for Responsive Politics (CRP), 81
Certified divorce financial advisors
  (CDFAs), 111, 196
Certified Elder Law Attorneys (CELA), 227
Certified financial analysts, 111
Certified financial planners, 111
Charitable giving. *See also*
  Volunteering
  for children, 172, 178
  as choice, 50
  in discovery process, 108
  family help vs., 100
  importance of, 76, 77–79, 240
  planning for, 111
  teaching about, 167, 169–170
  and values, 161
Child support, 14, 194
Childcare, 38, 138, 186, 231
Children, 163–180
  allowances for, 171–174
  charitable giving by, 172, 178
  credit cards for, 175–177
  and family values, 166–169
  financial advisors for, 178
  financial education for, 177–179
  grounded, 169–171
  in money confident homes, 165–166
  money conversations with, 178, 180
  money messages for, 179–180
  volunteering by, 170, 173
Community property, 155–157, 184
Compensation plans, 189
Context clues, 245
Covey, Stephen, 150, 256
COVID-19 pandemic, 79, 83, 220

Index

Credit card debt, 66–67, 189, 211
Credit cards:
　best practices for, 160
　budgeting for, 70
　for building credit scores, 16, 187, 189–190, 211
　and debit cards, 175–177
　and divorce, 184–185
　as documents, 225
　interest rates of, 16, 240
　legacy talks about, 232
　as leveraged asset, 65
　teaching children about, 164–165
　tracking, 47
　use of, 17–18
Credit scores, 15–18, 67, 160, 164, 176, 187
CRP (Center for Responsive Politics), 81

D

Death, 219–238
　conversations about, 223–224
　digital arrangements for, 232–233
　documents for, 225–226
　legacy talks about, 221–222
　and life insurance, 229–231
　planning for, 222–223
　representatives for, 228–229
　and trusts, 226–228
　and widowhood, 233–235
　and wills, 226–228
Death benefits, 231

Debit cards, 66, 165, 176
Debt:
　bad, 66, 235
　credit card, 66–67, 189, 211
　discussions about, 153
　in divorce, 189, 197
　educational, 69–72
　family governance over, 121
　in financial status, 185
　good, 58, 68, 235
　paying off, 243
　as property, 155–156
　stress over, 143
　student, 72–74
　transparency of, 161
Dementia, 201, 214–215
Diaz, Hernan, 256
Dickens, Charles, 256
Digital death, 232–233
Disability insurance, 142, 189
Discovery process, 108
Diversified portfolios, 60, 117–118
Divorce, 181–198
　advice on, 188–189
　advisors for, 191–192, 195–197
　communication in, 197–198
　and credit scores, 187–188
　discretion in, 184–185
　financial facts in, 183
　financial information in, 189–190
　financial status in, 185–186
　legacy plans in, 193–194
　preparing for, 182–189

Divorce (*Cont.*)
  process of, 189–198
  professional status in, 186–187
  and spousal support, 194–195
  teams for, 192–193
  timing of, 183–184
Divorce for Dummies (Ventura and Reed), 188, 256
Dow Jones industrial average, 119
Dreams papers, 30, 32, 34, 49
The Dutch House (Patchett), 256

E
Education savings, 71–72
Educational debt, 69–72. *See also* Student debt
Elder attorneys, 215, 227
Electing Women Bay Area, 77
Emergency funds:
  amounts in, 26–27
  definition of, 19–20
  for freelancers, 54
  for health issues, 174
  importance of, 8–9
  and insurance, 231
  for layoffs, 136–137, 158
  in money markets, 61
  as savings, 51
  teaching children about, 178
Emotional support systems, 196–197
Environmental, social, and governance portfolios, 118–119
Equal Credit Opportunity Act, 17

Equifax, 16
ETFs, 60, 62
Experian, 16

F
Facebook, 233
Family governance, 121
Family values, 166–169
Federal and State Income Tax Salary Calculator, 44
Fee-only financial planners, 109–110, 112, 196
Feedback, 129, 134, 186–187
Fidelity, 24, 25–26, 62, 120, 155
Fiduciary advisors, 111–114, 117, 193–194, 196, 229. *See also* Stockbrokers
Financial advisors:
  for children, 178
  consulting, 3, 22
  and death, 220, 225, 229
  definition of, 110–111
  and dementia, 214–215
  discussions about, 152, 154
  and divorce, 192, 195–196
  duties of, 109
  and education savings, 72
  information for, 189–190
  and insurance, 231
  interviewing, 114–121
  in legacy talks, 206
  money conversations with, 88
  of parents, 96, 99

self-management vs., 91
and structured gifts, 101
and trusts, 227
for widows, 233
Financial anxiety, 5, 54–55, 58, 64, 152
Financial novel clubs, 242–246
Financial planners, 37, 100, 109–110, 112, 115, 236
Financial planning, 14, 32, 111, 202
Financial policies, 46, 48–49
Financial status, 183
529 college funds, 79, 88, 100, 104, 179
501(c)3 organizations, 78
Fluvanna Political Equality Club, 80
401(k) plans:
  catch-up contributions to, 211
  contributing to, 26
  definition of, 22–24
  discussions about, 87–88, 154, 164
  enrolling in, 25
  as investment, 59
  and net earnings, 44
  for nonworking spouses, 21–22
  origin of, 209–210
  for partners, 91
  planning, 110
  researching, 27
  as retirement-only funds, 8, 179
  as savings, 51, 64
  solo, 37, 139
Freelancers, 36–37, 52–54, 139–142.
  See also Gig workers
Frugality, 168–169
Fun funds, 27, 50, 53

G
Gallup, 193
Gates, Bill, 9
Getting Unstuck (Butler), 38, 255
Gig workers, 24, 52, 53, 139–142.
  See also Freelancers
Glassdoor, 130, 133
The Good Will (Arnold), 237, 256
Google Inactive Account Manager, 233
Graham, Dawn, 38, 255
Great Expectations (Dickens), 240, 256
The Great Gatsby (Fitzgerald), 239–240, 256
Gross income, 26, 44, 158.
  See also Net income
Guardians, 228

H
Headhunters, 130
Health insurance, 19, 37, 44, 136, 142, 208, 212
Health savings accounts (HSAs), 132
Healthcare proxies, 228
Home ownership, 67–69
The House of Mirth (Wharton), 241, 256
Housing costs, 48, 57
How to Do Your Own Divorce in California (Sherman), 188, 256
HSAs (health savings accounts), 132

I

Ibarra, Herminia, 38, 255
Impact portfolios, 18
Incapacity documents, 225
Index funds, 26
Individual retirement accounts (IRAs):
   and alimony, 194
   catch-up contributions to, 211
   contributing to, 26
   definition of, 20–22
   discussing, 91
   401(k) vs., 22–24
   as investments, 59
   planning, 110
   researching, 25
   Roth, 21, 25, 95
   as savings, 51, 64
   SEP, 37, 139
   spousal, 21, 25
   tax breaks from, 44
Inheritances, 121, 147, 155, 185, 193, 203, 235
Instagram, 233
Insurance:
   disability, 142, 189
   in dreams papers, 45
   health, 19, 37, 44, 136, 142, 208, 212
   life, *see* Life insurance
   long-term care, 185, 202, 205, 211, 212–214
   planning, 111
Insurance agents, 231
Insurance brokers, 37, 231

Intelligent investor platforms, 220
Interest rates, 16, 18, 59, 61, 67, 177, 211
Internal Revenue Service (IRS), 21, 78, 102, 178
Investment benchmarks, 119, 141
Investment management agreements, 121–122
Investment philosophies, 117–118
IRAs, *see* Individual retirement accounts (IRAs)
Irrevocable trusts, 225. *See also* Trusts
IRS, *see* Internal Revenue Service (IRS)

J

Joint property, 155. *See also* Community property
Joy, spending with, 32, 49, 50, 63, 147, 219, 237
July, Miranda, 241, 256

K

Kedar, Sharon, 255
Kiyosaki, Robert, 69, 255

L

Layoffs, 136–137, 158
Lead advisors, 121
Legacy talks, 199–217
   about aging issues, 202–205
   beginning, 205–206
   about death, 221–222

about dementia, 214–215
in divorce, 193–194
emotions in, 206–207
with financial advisors, 206
about financial problems, 209–211
about insurance, 212–214
preparation issues in, 207–209, 211–212
Social Security in, 206, 212
Level two political organizing, 82
Life insurance:
discussions about, 224, 235
in divorces, 189, 193
legacy talks about, 212
permanent, 230
term, 229–230
understanding, 229–231
whole, 230
Lifestyle creep, 63–64
Lifestyle funds, 62
LinkedIn, 41, 130, 186
Liquidity, 57, 187, 198
Living wills, 225
Long-term care insurance, 185, 202, 205, 211, 212–214

M
McClintock, Mary Ann, 80
McElroy, Ken, 69, 255
Madoff, Bernie, 120
A Man on the Inside (television program), 214, 256
Managing up, 126–128, 130

Margo's Got Money Troubles (Thorpe), 256
Marital property, 155–157. *See also* Community property
Marriage, 145–161
allowances in, 159–160
budgets in, 159–160
conversation in, 151–152
financial sharing in, 157–159
money dates in, 5, 153–155, 159, 197, 201
money messages in, 146–148
personal financial history in, 149–151
property in, 155–157
transparency in, 161
Mary Poppins Returns (film), 145–146, 256
Maternity leave, 80, 137–138
Medicare, 44, 206, 211, 227
The Merchant of Venice (Shakespeare), 240, 256
Monday.com, 186
Money communication, 5, 164, 197, 247
Money confident homes, 165–166
Money conversations, 87–105
with children, 178, 180
during divorce, 182
with family, 77, 94–96, 99–101, 200, 203
about family support, 101–103
with friends, 103–105

Money conversations (*Cont.*)
   in money dates, 153
   numbers in, 92–94
   with partners, 151–152
   with siblings, 97–99
   starting, 5, 90–92
Money dates, 5, 153–155, 159, 197, 201
Money differences, 103–104
Money market funds, 8, 61, 211
Money Quotient, 149, 153
Money teams, 107–122
   fee-only financial planners in, 109–110
   fiduciaries in, 111–113
   financial advisors in, 110–111
   finding advisors for, 114–115
   interviewing for, 115–122
   stockbrokers in, 111–113
Moral values, 92, 171, 174
Mott, Lucretia, 80
Munger, Charlie, 170
Mutual funds, 60, 62, 65, 110

N

National Elder Law Foundation, 227
Net income, 19, 44, 47.
   See also Gross income
Nolo Press, 188

O

Oliver, Mary, 89
On My Own Two Feet (Thakor and Kedar), 255

P

Patchett, Ann, 256
PayPal, 53
Pension plans, 22–23, 185, 189, 206, 209
Permanent life insurance, 230
Political giving, 77, 80
Portfolios:
   assessment of, 230
   balanced, 23
   balanced growth, 59
   diversified, 59–60, 117–118
   emotions' effect on, 112
   environmental, social, and governance, 118–119
   examples of, 61
   family management of, 215
   fiduciary role in, 194
   impact, 18
   and long-term care, 213
   maintaining, 25
   planning, 58
   by robo-advisors, 62–63
   suggested, 110
   target funds vs., 63
Powers of attorney, 189, 215
Probate, 226–227
Professional status, 73, 186

R

Raises, 128–132
Retirement accounts, *see* 401(k) plans; IRAs (individual retirement accounts)

Index

Retirement savings:
  amount of, 24–25
  for children, 164
  discussions about, 89
  employee contributions to, 210
  401(k) plans as, 22–24
  goals for, 64
  IRAs as, 21, 22–24
  planning for, 14
  for widows, 219–220
Revenue Act, 209
Revocable trusts, 193, 225, 227, 228.
    See also Trusts
Rich Dad Poor Dad (Kiyosaki), 69, 255
Risk informed investments, 59
Robo-advisors, 62–63, 115
RocketMoney, 47
Roe vs. Wade, 3
Roth IRAs, 21, 25, 95
Russell 3000 Index, 119

S

Sacrifices, 9, 31, 49–50, 74, 168
Safety nets, 138, 230, 236
Salary negotiations, 71, 124–126, 129, 140
Salary ranges, 130, 133–1334
Sandwich generation, 200
Savings:
  automatic, 46
  budgeting for, 45, 51–52
  for children, 172
  cuts for, 47
  In dreams papers, 49–50
  for education, 71–72, 174
  emergency funds as, 20, 231
  examples of, 61
  financial advice for, 110, 118
  401(k) plans as, 51
  gifts for, 103
  and housing expenses, 48
  IRAs as, 51, 64
  and money messages, 149
  for multiple things, 51–52
  of parents, 209–210
  from raises, 125
  retirement, *see* Retirement savings
  spending of, 213
Scarcity mentality, 150, 168, 180
Schwab, 25–26, 62, 120, 154
Self-insuring, 213
SEP IRAs, 37, 139
Separate property, 155–157
The 7 Habits of Highly Effective People (Covey), 150, 256
Shakespeare, William, 240, 255
Single-person credit scores, 187–188
Slack, 186
"Sleep at night" factor, 60, 65, 134
Social Security:
  documents for, 226
  as financial information, 189
  legacy talks about, 206
  as payroll tax deduction, 44
  in retirement planning, 25, 211
  as sole source of income, 209

INDEX

Social Security (*Cont.*)
    as survivor benefit, 228
    women's income from, 20
Social Security Administration, 20, 25
Solo entrepreneurs, 36–37.
    See also Freelancers
Solo 401(k) plans, 37, 139
S&P 500, 119
Spending plans, 18, 45–46.
    See also Budgets
Spousal IRAs, 21, 25
Stanton, Elizabeth Cady, 80
Still Alice (film), 214, 256
Stock equity, 166
Stockbrokers, 111–114, 117, 208.
    See also Fiduciary advisors
Stress:
    budgeting for, 45, 55, 220
    from burnout, 142–143
    on children, 146, 174
    from conversations, 149
    cycles of, 129
    from debt, 65–66
    from divorce, 182, 184
    marital, 146, 197
    positive, 33
Structured gifts, 100–101
Student debt, 72–74. *See also*
    Educational debt
Sunk costs, 213
SUNY, 74
Support advisors, 121
Switchers (Graham), 38, 255

T

Take the Leap (Bliss), 38, 255
Target funds, 62–63
Tax deferred wealth, 22, 23
Term life insurance, 229–230
Thackeray, William Makepeace, 256
Thakor, Manisha, 255
Thorpe, Rufi, 256
Tipping, 168
Transfer on death (TOD) designation, 227
Transparency, 161, 178, 182
TransUnion, 16
Trust (Diaz), 241, 256
Trusts, 192–193, 225, 226–228
Tunneling, 150

U

UC Berkeley, 74
UCLA, 74
United States Bureau of Labor Statistics, 209
University of Michigan, 74
University of Virginia, 74
Unpaid, leave, 138

V

Value judgments, 161
Vanguard, 25, 62
Vanity Fair (Thackeray), 240, 256
Vegas rules, 245
Venmo, 53
Vesting periods, 23

Visuals, 50–51
Volunteering. *See also* Charitable giving
   by advisors, 115
   by children, 170, 173
   commitment to, 78–79
   importance of, 76–77
   level one, 82–83
   political, 80–81
Vulnerability, 192, 204, 206–208, 247–248

W
Wage replacement, 230
The Wall Street Journal, 241
Wharton, Edith, 241, 256
What Color is Your Parachute? (Bolles), 255
Whole life insurance, 230
Widowhood, 111, 220, 233–235, 242
Wills, 89, 193–194, 237

Women's suffrage movement, 79–80
Work environments, 123–143
   burnout in, 142–143
   and co-workers' salaries, 133–135
   freelancers in, 139–142
   and job change, 135
   layoffs at, 136–137
   managing up in, 126–128, 130
   and maternity leave, 137–138
   money conversations in, 132
   negotiations with bosses in, 124–126
   and raises, 128–132
Working Identity (Ibarra), 38, 255
Wright, Martha, 80

X
X, 233

Z
Zelle, 53